PADRE PIO

FATHER GABRIELE AMORTH

Padre Pio

Stories and Memories of My Mentor and Friend

Translated by Matthew Sherry

SAN FRANCISCO   IGNATIUS PRESS

Original Italian edition:
Padre Pio. Breve storia di un santo
© 2016 Centro Editoriale Dehoniano

Cover photo:
Padre Pio with Fr. Carmelo da Sessano and Two Nephews (1950s)
Courtesy of Casa Sollievo della Sofferenza,
San Giovanni Rotondo, Italy

Cover design by Enrique J. Aguilar

© 2021 by Ignatius Press, San Francisco
All rights reserved
ISBN 978-1-62164-440-8 (PB)
ISBN 978-1-64229-171-1 (eBook)
Library of Congress Control Number 2021931992
Printed in the United States of America ∞

CONTENTS

TRANSLATOR'S NOTE

As much as I enjoyed seeing Padre Pio in a new light, one of the nicer surprises in translating this book was Father Amorth's talent as a writer. The man knew how to tell a story.

He also knew how not to be a stickler when it comes to trivia. This is not an academic biography, and he makes a few mistakes on things like names and dates, just enough to keep the finger-pointers happy. I have noted some of these errors with footnotes and brackets, but they are generally unimportant.

Father Amorth knew Padre Pio better than any Pio scholar could. He writes from over twenty-five years of friendship. Readers who want food for heart and soul will be happy to have found this book.

Matthew Sherry
March 10, 2021

PREFACE

"Father Amorth, could you write a life of Padre Pio? You went to see him for so many years; you knew him well. You could also write down some personal memories no one else knows.... I could make do with something short, even just 150 pages ..."

I'll be honest: this has been no chore for me. I've enjoyed reviewing the life of my beloved spiritual father, to whom I went for twenty-six years, from 1942 to 1968; I've enjoyed thinking back on my meetings with him.

I really don't think I have anything new to say, nothing that hasn't already been said. But if this can be a small contribution to spreading the word about a great saint and enticing people to read other books about him, and above all his own writings, I'll gladly gird up for the job, although I know even now that the result will be very modest, far from equal to the figure of whom I speak.

Father Gabriele Amorth

ALREADY HE WAS DIFFERENT

The devotees of Padre Pio who go in ever greater numbers to visit Pietrelcina, eight miles from Benevento, find themselves in a delightful town of rolling hills at an elevation of just over one thousand feet. Many of the buildings are new; the streets are well kept; the hush is welcoming. It is only by exploring some of the little side streets that one recognizes the poor backwater of a century ago, when Padre Pio was born in Pietrelcina on May 25, 1887.

The three cramped little rooms on Vico Storto Valle that were his home still convey the poverty of his parents, Grazio Forgione and Maria Giuseppa Di Nunzio.

It was a hardscrabble life back then. Grazio, like many of his countrymen, had to go to America several times to scrape together enough for the family to get by on; Mama Peppa toiled from morning until evening, like all the moms in town. They were both illiterate, but they had great faith and that good practical sense that the Lord gives to the lowly. They had seven children, four of whom died young.[1]

There is not much we know about the childhood of Padre Pio, but what we do know is enough to understand that already he was different from the others: it was clear right from the start that the Lord had extraordinary plans for him. This may be distasteful to the modern mentality, which loves to see the saints as people just like the rest of us, full of defects, perhaps even going badly astray before resuming the uphill climb. We should not forget that the saints are, first of all, masterpieces of grace, so that at times, in addition to imitating the example they leave for us, we should admire the extraordinary plan of God in them, completely unique and unrepeatable. God had special plans for Padre Pio; it should come as no surprise if extraordinary events began to prepare him from his earliest childhood.

Going into the rustic Church of Saint Anne, one visits the little baptistry in which Padre Pio was baptized on the day after his birth. He was given the name Francesco, which would turn out to be prophetic in that little boy's decision to embrace the Franciscan life.

We know Francesco was very obedient as a child, so much so that his parents never had to raise

---

[1] C. Bernard Ruffin, *Padre Pio: The True Story* (Huntington, Ind.: Our Sunday Visitor, 2018) indicates that there were eight children, three of whom died young.—TRANS.

a hand against him. Very early on, he revealed his love of prayer and absolute intolerance of swearing and especially of blasphemy, which unfortunately was often on the lips of his young playmates.

A curious episode: When he was ten years old, he became ill and had to stay in bed for a month. One day, his mother prepared a big panful of fried peppers and then left the house for a bit. The sick boy got out of bed and, one after another, stuffed himself with all those peppers. The result? He got better!

Francesco received Confirmation when he was twelve, again at the Church of Saint Anne, on September 27, 1899; that may also have been when he received his First Communion. Meanwhile, he helped support the family by tending a few sheep. But his father had a sense of his intelligence and desire and got him an education. By the age of fifteen, Francesco had worked his way up to eighth grade; he had decided some time before to become a priest and to join the "friars with the beards", because he was an admirer of the good Fra Camillo, a simple friar with a long black beard who went around collecting alms.

But how had this decision come about? Here we begin to explore the extraordinary paths down which the Lord led Padre Pio. To the love of prayer he had soon added the love of penance, so much so that his mother repeatedly walked in on him while he was scourging himself. But the most unusual thing was that, from the earliest years of his life, starting at the age of four, the boy was favored with heavenly visions and already had to fight against the devil, who often made himself visible in obsessive and frightening ways.

We do not know much about these events because little Francesco thought they happened to everybody and did not talk about them. The apparitions were of his guardian angel, the Lord, the Blessed Mother, and others; the demons generally took the forms of wild animals, fearsome and threatening. This torment of demons, even in perceptible forms, and the comfort of divine apparitions would be—at least until he was pierced with the stigmata—an almost daily occurrence for Padre Pio.

The fight against the giant

Shortly before he joined the Capuchins in 1903, two things happened to Francesco at the age of fifteen that he always considered important and frequently discussed with his spiritual directors. They are two episodes that played a role of great significance in his life.

We know the first episode well enough, because Padre Pio recounted it a number of times. The version we will consider here comes from an account he wrote to his spiritual director, Father Agostino.

This was a vision he had. The youngster saw a radiant, handsome man who was beckoning to him:

"Come with me, because you are to fight as a valiant warrior." Together they went to a huge field. On one side were handsome men dressed in white garments; on the other were hideous men dressed in black, making them look like dark shadows. Francesco suddenly found himself facing a horrible man who was so tall that his head was in the clouds.

The radiant figure urged the youngster to fight the giant. Francesco pleaded with him to spare him from that contest, but the other said to him, "It is useless for you to resist. You have to scuffle with him. Take heart, enter the combat with trust, and fight courageously. I will be close by, helping you, and will not let him beat you."

The clash was terrible, but thanks to the help of that radiant figure, the giant was defeated and forced to retreat, followed by that multitude of repulsive men, who ran off hurling shrieks, curses, and deafening cries. But the other multitude broke into shouts of rejoicing and praise for the radiant figure who had helped Francesco in the unequal fight. At this point, the figure placed a crown of indescribable beauty on Francesco's head and then removed it, saying to him, "I am setting aside for you an even more beautiful crown, if you are able to fight against that giant. He will keep attacking you, but be fearless and fight him. I will always be near you so that you may always succeed in knocking him down."

Padre Pio's whole life was a continual fight against the devil, who attacked the priest and tried to keep him from saving souls. It was often an interior struggle but was sometimes an external attack. And when the priest, exhausted and covered with bruises and welts, finally got help from the other friars, he often confessed: "Thanks to heaven's help, I have always come out the winner." This episode was a very significant preview of Padre Pio's whole life.

The second episode, no less important, happened shortly after this. It is difficult to talk about this one because the Padre was always reticent about it. Several times he spoke or wrote about the essential point, which was that he had been chosen for "a very great mission". But he never wanted to get into the specifics. "A very great mission known only to you and to me", he wrote in a personal prayer. It is easy to guess that something had been revealed to him about his future apostolate. I gather this from a few signs; for example, from the great insistence with which he asked his superiors to be admitted to the ministry of confession.

By looking at his life and at the influence for good he exercised on a worldwide scale, we can well say he carried out "a very great mission". But we know nothing more about the revelation he received as a teenager.

These are two visions that profoundly marked the life of Padre Pio. In his battles against Satan, he would live over and over again that scuffle with the giant. And he would always keep in view the "very great mission" that the Lord showed to him. This would be a memory that would sustain him in the hard battles of his long life, both on account of his atrocious sufferings, such as the stigmata, and even more because of calumnies and canonical sanctions against him: he would offer everything to the Lord in fulfillment of that mission. This must have been the secret of his unwavering serenity.

Realism and hope. This is what he wrote to two of his spiritual daughters, Maria Gargani and Raffaelina Cerase:[2]

> Do not be afraid when the tempest rages, because the boat of your spirit will never go under. The heavens and the earth will change, but the Word of God that assures us that the obedient will sing of victory will not change; it will remain always written in indelible characters in the book of life: I will endure forever.[3]

> Let us always keep it before our eyes that here on earth is a place of combat and the crown is received in heaven; that here is the proving ground and the

[2] The complete letters of Padre Pio, in their original Italian, can be found in the four-volume *Epistolario Padre Pio da Pietrelcina*, eds. Melchiorre da Pobladura and Alessandro da Ripabottoni (San Giovanni Rotondo: Edizioni Padre Pio da Pietrelcina, 1971–1984). Hereafter, we will use the abbreviation "*Letters*".—TRANS.

[3] *Letters*, vol. 3.

prize is given up there; that here we are in a land
of exile and our true homeland is heaven, to which
we must continually aspire. So let us dwell with
living faith, with firm hope, and with ardent affection as long as we are wayfarers, so that one day,
when God pleases, we may dwell there in person.[4]

---

[4] *Letters*, vol. 2.

2

FRANCISCAN FRIAR

On January 6, 1903, when he was sixteen, Francesco said a heart-wrenching goodbye to his mom and entered the novitiate in Morcone, not far from Pietrelcina. He had twice already been the victim of unjust calumnies. I mention this only because Padre Pio—who was always of such chaste purity that one of his spiritual directors was moved to exclaim, "I am convinced he has never committed the smallest venial sin against this virtue"—on various occasions had to endure the most infamous accusations, which gave rise to humiliating investigations but always ended by bringing the truth of the matter to light.

Already during his first years at school, one of his classmates played a joke in bad taste that led to Francesco's being accused of having a crush on a girl. This earned him a painful beating from the teacher in the presence of his classmates. Once the truth came out, that poor teacher never got over the injustice he had done. Another time, shortly before Francesco entered the novitiate, a girl put a love note into his pocket without his noticing and then arranged things so that the note was found and the matter became known. This time, the one deceived was the parish priest, who gave Francesco the silent treatment and banned him from being an altar boy.

It was a heavy blow for Francesco, and he felt like an outcast even though he was innocent. This may have been a small foretaste of the much more serious unjust punishment he was to receive when he would be suspended from celebrating Mass in public and from hearing confessions. This time as well, the truth came out, because the culprit confessed the whole deception.

The parish priest, mortified that he had fallen into this childish trap and punished his favorite (he thought the world of Francesco) did his best to make up: he announced right away that he would charge nothing for the documents Francesco needed for entering the novitiate.

In addition to the pain of separation from his family and his town, the aspiring novice was not spared inner struggles: he had an "intellectual vision" through which he understood that his religious life would be a continual fight with that giant, as in the vision, and it was just as clear to him that this step was the beginning of the *lofty mission* to which God was calling him.

A few days after entering the novitiate, on January 22, he put on the Franciscan habit and was given the name Fra Pio of Pietrelcina. From that moment on, there was no more Francesco: only Pio. Francesco disappeared so thoroughly that one day the conscription officers would come looking for a certain Francesco Forgione, and no one would know who that was. But in exchange, another Francesco, the one from Assisi, had fully entered into Fra Pio of Pietrelcina, with his love for Christ and for his brothers, especially those sick in soul or body, and with his love of poverty. And he had also entered with a visible likeness, that of the stigmata, which would make Padre Pio an even more faithful copy of Saint Francis.

Padre Pio did not get off to a brilliant start in the religious life. His behavior and obedience were excellent, as was his jovial rapport with the other friars. But he was always sickly, and there was something strange about his studies. Overall these were good enough, never outstanding. But the strange part, as his classmates tell it, was that, although he always knew the material, no one ever saw him study.

Even during his years of theology studies, those who came to his cell would find him praying. It's not that he couldn't study, but that, as soon as he opened a book, he immediately felt caught up in the thought of God, a thought that was constantly with him.

There's no point in looking for some other explanation: Padre Pio lived to pray; prayer was his breath, his life. I would say that already before entering the friary, he was always absorbed in God, as he would continue to be, even when he was talking with someone or doing other things, although this did not distract him from his conversations and activities. But his prayer was uninterrupted and did not interfere with the other duties to which he had to attend.

As the years went by, his health problems took hold and continued to get worse until the doctors, seeing that none of their remedies were helping, recommended the young friar be sent back to Pietrelcina, where he could benefit from the healthful effects of his native air. There is no doubt the air of his town did him good, but this also highlighted a strange illness that no one has ever been able to explain and was a real puzzle for Padre Pio himself and for his superiors. What would happen is this: in Pietrelcina, Padre Pio was still in poor health but was at least able to eat a little and sustain himself; as soon as he went somewhere else, it seemed his stomach refused all food and he would throw everything up, unable to keep down even a spoonful of water. So his superiors felt they had no choice but to send him back to his hometown, and as soon as he set foot there, the problem went away.

In Pietrelcina

So it was that Padre Pio spent seven years in Pietrelcina, from 1909 to 1916, with a continual back and forth to one friary after another in the hope of being able to stay at one of them, only to be disappointed every time. As soon as he was a little better, his superiors would rush him off to another friary, but right away his stomach problem would flare up again and the local superior would have no choice but to send him back to his hometown. We can imagine what a trial it was for Padre Pio to yearn with every fiber of his being for the conventual life and be forced over and over again to leave it, and what a trial for his superiors as well, at a loss as to where they should send this friar who became ill no matter where he went.

Should he leave the Franciscan life and become a diocesan priest? There were some who were advising him to take this painful step, and Padre Pio's superiors were thinking along the same lines until a ruling by the Congregation for Religious gave the Capuchin friar permission to live outside the friary while continuing to wear the habit as a full-fledged member of the order.

What was life like for Padre Pio in the meantime? A great deal of prayer, continual meditation on the Lord's Passion, tears that flowed until his eyesight was weakened.

Nevertheless he continued his theology studies and, on August 10, 1910, was ordained a priest at the cathedral of Benevento. This was a decisive turning point in his life, because at that moment, there began what we can call without exaggeration "the mystery of Padre Pio's Mass", a mystery known to few and witnessed by even fewer in those early days. In fact, for six full years, Padre Pio continued to live his life of obscurity in Pietrelcina, occasionally interrupted by attempts to join a friary.

To give a better idea of the mystery of Padre Pio's Mass, I should add at this point that, along with his ordination, 1910 was also the year in which Padre Pio had offered himself as a "victim for sinners and for the poor souls in purgatory". Few understand the immense value and the immense risk involved in offering oneself as a victim. We have been saved by the sacrifice of Christ, to which we must make our own contribution with personal sacrifice. But the one who offers himself as a victim truly agrees to participate in this sacrifice in a heroic way and often pays for this generosity with tremendous sufferings for which there is no human remedy. This is why the faithful are advised not to make such commitments unless they are under the guidance of a skilled spiritual director, and spiritual directors are urged to exercise the greatest caution before allowing such vows to be made.

We do not know much about this period of Padre Pio's life. What we can say is that, apart from his home, there were three main spots in Pietrelcina where he spent his time. The first was the little Church of Saint Anne. This is where he celebrated

Mass, which could last for four hours and was therefore avoided by many. For Padre Pio, there was no place more important than this, and it was already the setting for something we are unable to understand. Further on, we will again consider the Masses of Padre Pio, the ones people from all over the world would come flocking to attend. Here this was not yet the case; just the opposite.

Although Father Giuseppe Orlando attended some of Padre Pio's Masses, there is little he can say: "His Holy Mass is an incomprehensible mystery." In the light of what was shown to us later, we are able to affirm that from the time of his priestly ordination, the Mass of Padre Pio was truly a reliving of the Passion of Christ.

Two other places in Pietrelcina where the Padre passed the hours have become pilgrimage destinations for his devotees. At the end of Via Salita Castello is an old "little tower". This could bear witness to the prayerful solitude of this man who was all for prayer, all for union with his Lord. The last key spot is an elm on the hill of Piana Romana, not far from the Forgione home. It was there that little Francesco would take refuge in prayer and study, in the shade of that tree. And there, as a priest, he spent long hours in prayer, in meditation on the Passion of the Lord, until his relatives decided to treat him by building a little hut with a cot in it so he could spend the night there during the summer.

It was only after the publication of Padre Pio's letters to his spiritual directors (to Father Benedetto until 1922 and then to Father Agostino) that we learned something about how the Padre spent his days and nights: continual prayer, battle with demons, apparitions or interior visions. To the sufferings due to poor health and fights with the devil were added other sufferings that the Lord sent his servant for the fulfillment of his mission, as sanctifier of souls.

Already in 1910, while he was praying beneath the elm, Padre Pio received the stigmata in invisible form. A chapel has been built on the spot to commemorate this event. He often suffered the piercing of the heart and almost once a week was subjected to the scourging and to the crowning with thorns. If, during his childhood and even more so in the years when he was preparing for the priesthood, his constant meditation was on the Lord's Passion, now this was no longer a matter of simply meditating on the sufferings of Christ but of living them in his flesh. And it was just the beginning!

This brings us to the conclusion of this phase of his life, which we could call the "seven years in Pietrelcina". When he joined the Franciscans in 1903, a voice had said to him clearly: "Become holy and make others holy." The pain of having to live outside the friary was mitigated by the knowledge that he had the approval of his superiors and was within the bounds of canon law, thanks to the rescript from the Congregation for Religious allowing him to remain in Pietrelcina. He could still celebrate Mass at the little Church of Saint Anne, even if his eyesight had become so weak that he had to get permission to celebrate the Mass of the Blessed Mother or for the deceased, relying on his memory instead of having to make the effort to read. They were years characterized by a daily fluctuation between diabolical harassment and exquisite ecstasies. All of this lasted until February 17, 1916.

3

FINAL DESTINATION:
SAN GIOVANNI ROTONDO

Padre Pio obtained the faculty of hearing confessions relatively late, as this is usually granted shortly after priestly ordination—if anything, subject to passing an examination in moral theology. From Pietrelcina, he provided spiritual direction for a few persons who had been entrusted to him, by means of written correspondence. This too, spiritual direction by letter, would be one of the Padre's trademarks. One of his charges was a very kind elderly lady from Foggia, Raffaelina Cerase, a true chosen soul. She became gravely ill and insistently told her acquaintances among the Capuchins of Foggia about her desire to meet Padre Pio before she died.

It was a very understandable desire; it was a request for a great act of charity. It also turned out to be, at last, the right opportunity, so eagerly awaited by his superiors, to get Padre Pio out of his isolation in

Pietrelcina. Both his spiritual director and the provincial superior agreed that the Padre should make this visit to Foggia—they expected it to be just a quick trip—to tend to the dying woman.

So Padre Pio (who meanwhile was going through a period of tremendous dryness, a true night of the spirit) laboriously made his way to Foggia. After settling into the dirt-poor friary, he dedicated himself to tending to the sick woman, who died a holy death on March 25, the feast of the Annunciation. At the friary of Saint Anne, as that little Capuchin community was called, Padre Pio did not relapse into the vomiting that deprived him of all nutrition, so he stayed, happy to be living in community at last and to share the great poverty of his fellow friars.

Padre Pio's stay at Saint Anne was anything but peaceable. Although the friars greatly appreciated the presence of a priest so dedicated to prayer and as cheerful and pleasant as could be at recreation time, disturbing things were happening. Often, especially in the evening, there were noises and explosions that left those poor friars terrified. Padre Pio apologized to the superior and explained: the devil was testing him with every sort of trial, but he fought back and always won. Yet he would be covered with sweat and so exhausted that the other friars would have to help him change clothes. He always remained serene, however, and tried to transmit his serenity to the others.

It should be added that his presence did not go unnoticed by the people. He was immediately sought out as a confessor and a spiritual director, which brought growing numbers of the faithful to the friary.

But on July 28, something else happened that could have been insignificant and instead was of decisive importance. The superior of the friary of San Giovanni Rotondo passed through Foggia. Seeing how Padre Pio was suffering from the severe heat, he asked if he wanted to go up to San Giovanni for a few days. Padre Pio accepted gladly, not thinking he was to stay in San Giovanni for fifty-two years.

The friary of Santa Maria delle Grazie

In 1916, San Giovanni Rotondo had absolutely nothing to recommend it. It was a very poor little town, like so many out-of-the-way towns of the Italian south, with a few thousand inhabitants. Isolated on account of the lack of roads, it had no electricity, running water, or sanitation. A mile from the town there was a mule track that led up to the Capuchin friary, two thousand feet above sea level. Bleak was the friary; even bleaker was the countryside of rocky hills dotted with wild shrubs. The only lovely thing, in the little church all made of arches and vaults, was Santa Maria delle Grazie

[Our Lady of Graces], reigning from the center of the main altar, who had given the church and friary their name.

It was here that Padre Pio arrived on July 28, 1916, in the company of the superior, almost as if for a break of a few days, to get away from the sweltering heat of Foggia. In fact, the Padre relished the fresh air right away, so much so that he was the one who asked the superior for permission to extend that stay for a little while. He was feeling a bit of physical relief, but there were other reasons too, things Jesus was saying to him. It is difficult to know if it was revealed to him immediately that he would spend the rest of his life there, but he was certainly alerted that this was the place of his apostolate.

He was happy to be there, and the friars were happy to have him. But the arrangement was not to everyone's liking. Deep within, Padre Pio was subjected to a tremendous battle. He felt "exposed to the fury of Satan", who surely did not want to see him in that place. The Padre felt assaulted by temptations against the faith that were so strong that he was prompted to write, "What a mystery I am to myself!" So sure in guiding souls, he felt then, as he always did thereafter, so weak and uncertain when it came to his own person.

It was not only the evil one that disturbed Padre Pio in the apparent quiet of San Giovanni. There was the first great war. The Padre was also called to arms, and until March 16, 1918, his life was a series of journeys and returns, of medical visits and convalescent furloughs. He had fevers so high that they broke the thermometer; one bath thermometer recorded a temperature of over 118 degrees Fahrenheit. His strange symptoms baffled the doctors, who honestly admitted they had no idea what was happening.

It was a very hard time for him on account of the physical rigors to which he was subjected, but even more so on account of the language and behavior of the other recruits and above all because so often it was not possible to celebrate Holy Mass. In exchange, he got to know much better that world for whose sake he was driven to sacrifice himself.

At the friary, he was entrusted with a particular task: he was the spiritual director for the *"fratini"*, the young aspirants to the Capuchin order studying with the friars. Padre Pio dedicated himself to them wholeheartedly: hearing confessions, fighting the devil on their behalf, and, in keeping with his total generosity, offering himself to the Lord as a victim for them. But soon the friar had another duty. So many people began going to him for confession that, before long, this took up the whole morning. The Padre heard confessions, gave spiritual direction, and offered guidance by letter.

His torments did not come only from the devil. The Lord had special plans for that friar and, amid an abundance of spiritual consolations, was preparing him to become ever more a visible sign in his image. From August 5–7, 1918, Padre Pio underwent almost without interruption the phenomenon that in mysticism is called "transverberation".

On August 9, 1912, he had written the following to Father Agostino:

> I also feel, my father, that love will overcome me in the end; the soul runs the risk of parting from the body because on earth it cannot love Jesus enough. Yes, my soul is wounded with love for Jesus; I am sick with love; I constantly feel the bitter pain of that ardor that burns and does not consume. Suggest to me, if you can, the remedy for the current state of my soul. Here is a feeble image of what Jesus is doing in me. As a stream carries along with it into the depth of the seas all that it encounters in its course, so also does my soul plunge into the boundless ocean of Jesus' love, without any merit of my own and without being able to explain it to myself, pulling after it all of its treasures.

And on August 12 of the same year:

> I was in church making my prayer of thanksgiving after Mass when, all of a sudden, I felt my heart wounded by a dart of fire so searching and ardent that I believed I would die of it. I have no words to make you understand the intensity of that flame; I

am even powerless to explain it to myself. Do you believe it? The soul, victim of these consolations, becomes mute. It seemed to me that an invisible force was immersing me entirely in the fire.... My God, what fire!... One second more, my soul would have separated from the body.... It would have gone away with Jesus.[1]

It was as if someone from heaven, with a long, sharp-pointed iron blade, were piercing his heart with stab after stab. From that moment on, the Padre felt this wound always open and bleeding, never to be healed.

[1] *Letters*, vol. 1.

4

THE STIGMATA

The first few months of 1918 were filled with sadness. The war and the Spanish flu had ravaged the population and the friaries. I would be remiss not to mention among the victims of that epidemic two of the three visionaries of Fatima, Francisco and Jacinta. The friary of Santa Maria delle Grazie had been reduced to three friars: Father Paolino, the superior; Fra Nicola, the mendicant; and Padre Pio, who also caught the Spanish flu, thank heavens in a less virulent strain, although he had to stay in bed from September 5 to 17. And there was the little group of young aspirants.

On the morning of Friday, September 20, the feast of the Stigmata of Saint Francis, Padre Pio was praying alone after Mass, in the choir stalls. Almost without realizing it, he was lulled to sleep, with a sense of complete peace. Suddenly there came before him the crucifix that still stands on the balustrade of the little choir area.

But this time, the figure on the crucifix looked the same as the one who on August 5 had transverberated his heart. With one difference: blood was dripping from his hands, feet, and heart. He then suddenly disappeared.

Padre Pio, who had been terrified at this sight, felt himself being torn open in those same places, in his hands, feet, and heart; he felt them being pierced and realized he was bleeding heavily.

He crawled to his cell and did what he could to bandage the wounds.

Later he would write to his spiritual director about the sentiments he felt and would continue to feel: torment, condemnation, humiliation, confusion. He could find no peace and did not know how to behave with his fellow friars and with others. In vain he would plead with the Lord with all his might, "Leave the pain, increase it if you will, but take from me the visible wounds. Give me the grace of not letting them be seen!"

The sense of confusion was oppressive, unbearable. He lived through "horrible and sad days", feeling that in the sight of God he was "a revolting and loathsome monster". And yet, in spite of these supplications and tears, he never took back his fiat.

These are clearly not the sentiments of someone who has sought out the stigmata, much less of someone who has marked himself with them artificially. This needs to be said right away because these would be the first suspicions and the first accusations.

Despite all of Padre Pio's efforts to hide what had happened, his superior, Father Paolino, easily spotted the wounds—he could have missed them only if he had been blind!—and told the provincial, who immediately urged absolute secrecy. But how could such a plain fact be concealed? The hands, covered with fingerless gloves, from which a stream of blood sometimes poured, and, in any case, uncovered during the celebration of the Mass; the halting steps, the face more racked with suffering than usual ... People are not stupid. Those signs were noted, the rumors began, and before long, the news had spread like wildfire. Soon members of the press came nosing around from Naples, from Italy, from the world.

Then for the Padre there began the calvary of the medical visits. Dr. Luigi Romanelli thoroughly examined the wounds on five occasions, made a detailed description of them, and concluded that "scientifically they [were] absolutely inexplicable".

Next up was Dr. Bignami, who wanted at all costs to show this was a temporary phenomenon with a human explanation. He subjected Padre Pio to an eight-day treatment of scar formation, under the strict supervision of four friars who had to put a seal over the bandages each time. The famous professor was sure that, at the end of the treatment, the lesions would be healed over.

What happened instead was that when the bandages were definitively removed at the end of the prescribed eight days, the wounds were bloodier and more open than ever.

Then it was Dr. Giorgio Festa's turn, again at the behest of the Capuchin superiors, who ordered the Padre, under the vow of obedience, to submit to those visits and treatments. Needless to say, Dr. Festa as well not only ascertained and stated that those wounds were scientifically unexplainable, but he went on to become a strenuous defender of Padre Pio.

Meanwhile the Padre, without paying any heed to the medical studies and to the confusion of the journalists, continued to celebrate his long Masses, to hear confessions, and to direct souls in person or in writing. He kept the pain and humiliation to himself, trying harder than ever to hide the wounds and the suffering they caused him.

The very first time I went to see him, I was told by someone who spent whole months at a time with Padre Pio, "Don't be fooled. The Padre suffers atrociously from the stigmata, but he is a true artist in being able to conceal this."

At this point, allow me to present a personal memory concerning the stigmata of Padre Pio, this priest who suffered and saved souls but always met with opposition, even if in good faith (to protect him, to prevent fanaticism, etc.) from the Capuchin and ecclesiastical authorities. I'm jumping ahead to 1958. This was at the height of the second decade of tremendous persecution aimed at Padre Pio. The Capuchin superiors were prohibiting their charges from going to see the Padre, and the ecclesiastical authorities looked askance at those who organized visits to San Giovanni Rotondo or even hit them with disciplinary measures. The people were at a loss: If the Lord had given Padre Pio that visible sign of the Passion, wasn't it an open invitation to seek him out, as a model in the imitation of Christ?

During those years, I was writing every week for *Famiglia Cristiana*. The editor, my fellow Pauline Father Zilli, knew I was going to see Padre Pio on a regular basis. He said to me, "It is time to speak clearly. Write a balanced and solid article; I will publish it on the first two pages, the top spot in the whole magazine."

So I wrote my article, which was published on November 23, 1958, with a somewhat provocative headline: "So Then, Should We Believe Padre Pio or Not?" It was decidedly against the grain. I am not presenting it because of the splash it made at the time, but for a much more important reason that I will explain at the end. (It will be noted that I respond to a question from a reader who was disturbed by the fact that her associate pastor had claimed Padre Pio was fabricating everything and that Pius XI had spoken out against him. The reader had also asked if there were any existing criteria to go by.) Here is the article:

One cannot start with the assumption that the stigmata are impossible. In the history of the Church, there have been around 340 persons who have had them; roughly eighty of these are canonized, so there is no doubt as to their goodness and sincerity. Some try to understand why God would send these wounds, what meaning they hold. Probably to remind men about the redemptive value of suffering and to invite them to meditate on the Passion of the Savior. But it cannot be denied that, in the subject who bears them, they can indicate a fuller conformity to the image of Jesus. Perhaps this aspect, which is clear to us, escapes Padre Pio.

For Padre Pio, the stigmata are something not his own; they do not have to do with him but serve only to recall the wounds of the Lord. This is why he allows them to be kissed, just as he would offer a sacred image to be kissed. I would say he himself has a veneration for them.

In reality, they are an image of the Crucified, not carved in wood or painted on canvas but impressed upon his living flesh.

The Church has spoken out openly in favor of the historical truth and supernatural character of the stigmata of Saint Francis, who was the first to receive from God this seal of suffering and of conformity to Jesus Christ. Since then, there has been ever greater clarification—especially in recent times—of the criteria according to which it is possible to recognize or not recognize the presence of real stigmata, meaning they have a supernatural character. In theory, the principles are clear, but, of course, in practice an abundance of caution must be used in applying them, especially when it comes to someone who is still alive.

In spite of this, we believe that, concerning Padre Pio, a judgment can be made. Other illustrious theologians have already preceded us in this: we all realize for a fact that this is not a matter of a "newcomer" of whom it is legitimate to be distrustful. This is instead a matter of a very well-known person, under the closest scrutiny, seventy-one years old (Padre Pio was born on May 25, 1887), who has borne the stigmata for more than forty years. So there is already the evidence of time that, albeit not in a definitive way, legitimizes a judgment on a personal basis.

On the *fact* that Padre Pio has the stigmata there is no disagreement; there are conclusive and published medical proofs; it is a truth that can be verified at any time. Let us see instead if we can maintain that the origin of these wounds is supernatural. There are five criteria on which this judgment must be based:

1. The stigmata must be genuine wounds, important changes in the tissues, and placed where the wounds of Christ were (approximately: since these are *mystical* wounds, it does not matter, when it comes to the secondary details, if they reflect historical truth or common belief; so it does not matter if the wounds are in the wrist or in the palm, if the wound in the side is on the right or

the left). Natural wounds, instead, can be found on any part of the body.

2. They must appear instantaneously; in general, they bring the sharpest pain on days that recall the Passion of the Lord, such as on Fridays and during Holy Week. The pain from natural wounds is instead affected by weather; in any case, it has no correlation with the liturgical calendar.

3. In true stigmata, there is an absence of pus, putrefaction, fetid odor, and so forth. Natural lesions that do not heal quickly, however, especially if they are not disinfected, produce pus and can become gangrenous.

4. The stigmata are accompanied by continual hemorrhages. Not so other wounds.

5. The stigmata remain unchanged in spite of all medical treatment; they are not affected by therapeutic remedies or suggestion; they can even last for many years. Other wounds respond to treatment and form scars.

The wounds of Padre Pio meet all of these requirements.

It is true that various rationalist physicians have tried to come up with natural mechanisms (suggestion, hysteria, fixation, etc.) to explain stigmatization. But they are the same ones who, on account of their intellectual affiliation, deny the existence of supernatural phenomena: their arguments do not hold up scientifically. All the more so in that, if these were matters of pathology, the subjects should show in many ways that they are hysterical or abnormal (as, in reality, happens when it comes to these things). Instead, types like Padre Pio, full of good sense and healthy activity, show themselves to be in excellent psychological condition. There is an anecdote about a young American physician who said to the Padre, "I do not believe in your stigmata; they came because you were thinking hard about the wounds of the Crucified." And the good friar answered him, with a kindly smile, "Attaboy! Now go think intensely about an ox, and before you know it, you'll be sprouting horns." The quip was enough to make that rookie doctor change his mind.

If matters are this clear, why doesn't the Church speak out? Because there is another reason. The Lord gives these graces to subjects who practice the most heroic virtues and who usually have other supernatural gifts, such as ecstasies, bilocation, and so forth. We should take note of this: rather than seeing the stigmata as proof of holiness, the Church expects to see holiness as proof of the stigmata. And holiness does not consist of special gifts from God, which could also be given solely for the sake of the faithful; it lies instead in the exercise of the virtues to a heroic degree and with perseverance to the very end. This is why it can be verified only after death; as long as we are alive, we are all in danger of falling at any moment, no matter what level of union with God we may have reached.

This is why the Church is not speaking out. But this does not mean we cannot form a personal conviction about Padre Pio: we have every right to do so. It is licit for us to admire the wonders of grace in him, just as it is licit "not to believe"; it is not a sin! But even in this personal judgment, we must not follow our whims or moods. We find this rule suggested in the Gospel: "The plant is known by the fruits; if the fruits are good, the plant is good." So we should make our judgment by observing the patience of Padre Pio, his charity, his acceptance of suffering, his holy life dedicated only to doing good.

There is no one who does not know about conversions, returns to the Church, lives transformed by the encounter with the Padre. These are facts that cannot leave us indifferent, even more so than the healings and so forth, even if we sometimes feel annoyed by the excessive enthusiasm of some or the fanaticism of others.

Under Pius XI, a certain visit was made to the Padre, and a negative judgment was expressed. But this was not an official judgment, much less an infallible one. It was one opinion among many, expressed by a physician who was immediately called a jackass by another doctor. With all due respect, Pius XI had nothing to do with these matters. Though it is known that on the day of the beatification of Saint Thérèse of Lisieux, Padre Pio was seen at St. Peter's (even though he remained in San Giovanni Rotondo at the very same time), a well-known monsignor who witnessed this told the pope, adding that Father Orione [now Saint

Luigi Orione] had seen him too. And the pope replied, "If Father Orione saw too, I believe it."

In conclusion, since we are free, let us indeed think with our heads, but using reason, which should always characterize man. It is absurd, after so many years of evidence and so many authoritative testimonies, to deny verified facts and toss a hasty opinion at a man like Padre Pio. He is a man of God, a "great priest", in the full exercise of a ministry that has worldwide appeal.

Some may be satisfied with this. Those who, moreover, recognize other supernatural charisms in him and deem him an instrument of the Lord for extraordinary graces should think about the masses of faithful who flock to San Giovanni, about the prominent ecclesiastical and civilian figures who go to him, and they will feel themselves in good company.

Forty years later

Forty years have gone by since I wrote this article, in difficult times. There is nothing in it I have to correct. Instead, I would like to tell the reader why I ascribe such importance to that article. In addition to the value of what it affirms, there was a follow-up I have never told anyone about. Not long afterward, I went to San Giovanni Rotondo, where I was met by my dear friend Father Mariano, who can still bear witness to these facts. He was the one who introduced me to the superior, Father Carmelo of Sessano, who was Padre Pio's superior for six years and his spiritual son for fifty. So he knew the Padre very well.

I had that issue of *Famiglia Cristiana* with me, and I offered it to Father Carmelo, but he said to me right away, "That article, we've all read it here." And I: "Did you like it? Did you find it faithful?" Father Carmelo: "We all liked it. We agreed with it. It was clearly written by someone who was holding himself back, who wanted to say so much more." He looked at me with a little smile of satisfaction, as if he still had another pleasant surprise for me. He continued: "I showed the magazine to the Padre; he knew we had already read it and asked me for it. I brought it to his room, and then he gave it back to me the next day." I was very anxious and asked right away, "What did Padre Pio say?" Father Carmelo: "Nothing. He didn't say anything. He was so serene that I understood one thing with certainty: in that article he didn't find anything to criticize. He would have told me." I couldn't have been more pleased.

But are the stigmata of Padre Pio really so important? Should they be given so much attention in a brief biography like this one? In my view, their importance is immense, because the Lord gave the stigmata to Padre Pio so that they would be like an authentic calling card from him: behold the priest of Christ Crucified.

Of course, we were all going to Padre Pio for his Mass and confession, not to see the stigmata. But to know that this stigmatized priest, the very first (we know of no other priests with the stigmata so far), bore the seal that made him not only a sharer in the Passion but almost a reproduction of the Passion of Christ—this was what drew people to him.

If the Lord had not wanted to give Padre Pio this obvious appeal, he would have left the stigmata invisible; in making them visible, bleeding, analyzable, he wanted to make plain to the world the true identity of this man, his minister, imitator, mirror. It is no use trying to hide what God wants to be apparent.

And when the purpose was gone, the stigmata disappeared too, even more mysteriously than they had come. After fifty years: a Friday in 1918, a Friday in 1968.

5

FROM ALL OVER THE WORLD

When Padre Pio received the stigmata, there was already a certain group of persons who were going to him for confession and spiritual direction. In addition to the friars, these were the persons who found out about what had happened and brought others running from San Giovanni and the nearby towns.

When the news spread even more widely through the press, people started coming from all over Italy and from abroad. So that sleepy little town in the region of Gargano, so troublesome to get to and without any of the resources for accommodation, all at once became a center for pilgrimages that grew ever more numerous during the Padre's lifetime, and even more so after his death.

And yet those worthy Capuchins did all they could to keep this from happening, exerting themselves with a zeal that was truly excessive. The first effort was directed toward keeping the facts secret. The publication of Dr. Festa's conclusions was prohibited, and as far as it lay in their power, the Capuchins tried to stem the tide of pilgrims.

We should realize the difficulty and the strain to which they were subjected, under a constant bombardment of requests, often accompanied by letters of recommendation, always aimed at the same goal: we want to talk with Padre Pio. To one side, there were superiors commanding the strictest silence; to the other, there were throngs of the faithful pressing them with continual requests—at some point, it is only human to run out of patience.

I recall very well that in those first years, I was not the only one who came away from San Giovanni enthusiastic over Padre Pio and at the same time disgusted with the rudeness of the friars and, perhaps even more so, of certain persons around Padre Pio who had taken it upon themselves to control the traffic however they saw fit, sometimes with rather awkward results.

It can at least be stated with complete certainty that it was not the friars who encouraged the visits to the Padre. When the news stories began to come out (the first newspaper to cover Padre Pio was *Il Mattino* in Naples, on June 20, 1919), they brought a hailstorm of reproaches down on those poor friars, as if it had been their fault.

The provincial, Father Benedetto, went so far as to write to the superior of the friary of San Giovanni: "I prohibit *sub gravi* [on pain of mortal sin!]

communication with anyone about the events that
have taken place or will take place." He ordered
that no one be given the photo that had been taken
of Padre Pio in which his stigmata were clearly on
display. There was to be no talk about his fever,
which rose as high as 119.3 degrees, or about the
healings and conversions attributed to him. He did
at least recognize, however, the significance of the
medical findings and the exemplary nature of Padre
Pio's life.

Padre Pio celebrated his long Masses and heard
confessions, sometimes for more than sixteen hours
a day. So even those who went to him out of curiosity got caught up in his daily activities, which meant
spending long hours in church or in the sacristy,
and, like it or not, they ended up praying. Believ-
ers and the incredulous, bishops and other prelates,
rich and poor: it was a mad dash to the feet of him
whom Benedict XV called with conviction "a true
man of God".

The day, the life, of Padre Pio was characterized,
on the outside, by a stressful monotony. Fifty-two
years in the little church of a little friary, between
altar and confessional, then the choir area and his
cell. One could say he inhabited a few dozen square
feet of space. No trips, no preaching, no particular
functions or duties of any special regard. No vacation, ever. Nothing but crowds with their relent-
less demands—after all, they had come from so far

away, with such inconvenience and the burden of many sufferings.

In addition, there were Padre Pio's inner struggles. Especially from 1910 to 1922, he experienced what the great mystics call "the dark night", as his letters to his spiritual directors bear witness. He lived in constant agony, as if he were always being crucified.

We can understand very well the answer he gave to a poor woman who was venting to him about her many sufferings; at a certain point, she exclaimed, "I understand that the agony of Jesus on the cross was a suffering greater than any other. But at least it lasted only three hours." Padre Pio looked at that woman with an eye of compassion and said to her slowly, from the depths of his heart and from the depths of his personal experience, "But don't you know that Jesus is in agony until the end of the world?"

Yes, there were many *signs* in addition to the stigmata: the odor of sanctity, bilocation, reading consciences, prophecies, healings, conversions—so many incidents that were passed along by word of mouth and often ended up written down in his biographies. It must be said that during the long spans of time people spent outside the church, they would talk, and everyone had something to say. Then back home, there would be someone else who had seen Padre Pio, and they would start to talk about him, about what each had experienced, a topic that seemed inexhaustible.

It is significant that those who went to Padre Pio were bound to go back; those who went to Padre Pio realized that their visit, that Mass, that confession, had made a profound impression upon them, creating in a certain way a lasting bond that kept them wanting to return.

My first visit

The first time I went to see Padre Pio was in August 1942; I had no idea I would be going back there for twenty-six years. It was wartime, so there was less of a crowd than there had been before and would be again in the years to come. I remember the slow train that took me from Naples to the station in Foggia. Come to think of it, the station wasn't there at the time; it had been bombed, and all that was left were the tracks.

I was accompanied by my old parish priest, Father Andrea Barbolini, who had offered to pay for the trip. As soon as we got onto the bus for San Giovanni Rotondo, we met a lady who was willing to let us stay at her home. There were no hotels or boarding houses, but plenty of homes with a warm welcome for pilgrims. These did not cost very much, as Padre Pio would reprimand anyone who took advantage of the pilgrims. There was so much cordiality in these poor, simple dwellings. I remember there was electricity, and there were pitchers of water and basins for washing; best not to talk about the latrine arrangements.

The morning began at around 4:00 with the Padre's Mass starting at 5:00, but I was up by 3:30. The walk to the friary was just over a mile, with a biting wind that cut to the bone. The mule track had been replaced with a paved road, an order said to have come from Mussolini. The door of the little church was locked, and those who had gotten there before me said it would be opened five minutes before the hour, just in time to get in and attend Mass from the beginning.

It had been pointless for me to get there early, although there were others who had arrived even before I had.

How cold it was in front of that church! I was to suffer that cold many more times, with no shelter from a wind that whistled through the rocks on the hillside. I remember one winter when we stood huddled together like sheep, hoping in vain that the friar sacristan would have pity on us and open a bit earlier than usual. Not a chance.

Once inside, I hurried with the other men to the sacristy, behind the main altar. The Padre had already come down and begun to vest himself slowly for Mass, assisted by his spiritual sons who were already practiced in this and by a Capuchin friar who acted as his assistant. When he was vested and had the sleeves of his alb almost covering his hands, he took off the fingerless gloves, with that friar at the ready to secure them in his satchel.

After a few minutes, the little church was full, so the main altar had been prepared for the celebration. Padre Pio usually celebrated at the side altar dedicated to Saint Francis. I was one of those who received Communion from the Padre, and I remember his attentiveness but also his fatigue on account of that Mass, which lasted an hour and forty-five minutes. After a brief thanksgiving came the confessions of the men in the sacristy, then of the women in the church. At the very end, I saw everyone lining up on both sides of the corridor that the Padre would pass through on his way back to the friary.

He walked past slowly, while everyone tried to kiss his hand or to place it on their heads in a gesture of blessing. And at the same time, there was an uninterrupted chorus, as he neared the door: "Padre Pio, pray for my son; he's dying"; "Padre Pio, I'm losing my eyesight; pray for me"; "Padre Pio, I had an accident at work; pray that I may be able to go back"; "Padre Pio, my wife has a fever that the doctors do not understand; pray ..."

When he got to the door, Padre Pio turned around, gave a blessing with broad gestures, and went back to the friary. On one of my subsequent

visits, while he was turning around to give the blessing, I heard something that must have come forth
from him a number of times, because I have also
read it in some of his biographies: "All have their
cross; all ask that it be taken away. But if they knew
how precious it is, they would be asking that it be
given to them."

Yet he assured everyone of his prayers, either by
word or by gesture.

In the afternoon, everyone was back in church
for confessions and prayer. When Padre Pio left
and the church was locked, one could say the day
had come to an end. During that first visit, I had
the chance to exchange a few words with "Uncle
Grazio", Padre Pio's dad. He was sitting on the
curb that enclosed a big tree in front of the friary; I
found him in good spirits but bent more on his own
thoughts than on talking.

I also remember well a little portico that stood
perpendicular to the church, where Padre Pio sometimes celebrated Mass outdoors starting in 1954; it
was there that I was once invited by the friar who
served for him.

I did not become an enthusiast on that first visit.
The advice Padre Pio gave me, which was what I
had gone to him for, was full of good sense but com-
monplace, the kind any priest could have given me.

It had none of the extraordinary that I was crav-
ing. This taught me a lesson that still comes in handy

today: no one has the Holy Spirit in his pocket, and even the holiest persons and those most endowed with charisms receive particular gifts from the Lord one at a time, as he sees fit, so that, for everything, thanks may be given to none but the Lord.

But the memory of that Mass remained etched in my mind. I realized that even if for no other reason, I would have to go back for that.

6

WHOSE SINS YOU
SHALL FORGIVE ...

"What does Padre Pio do?"

"Your Holiness, he takes away the sins of the world."[1]

This simple exchange between Pius XII and Manfredonia archbishop Andrea Cesarano during an *ad limina* visit in April 1947 tells us quite clearly what was the main apostolic activity of the stigmatized friar. I am convinced that in that 1903 revelation in which the young Francesco, who was about to join the Capuchins, was shown that a *lofty mission* had been set aside for him, he was being told in advance about his future activity as a confessor. Otherwise, it is difficult to explain how in the world someone like Padre Pio, who asked for nothing and accepted

---

[1] Unless otherwise noted, the quotations presented in this chapter are taken from *I quaderni della Casa Sollievo della Sofferenza*, supplement to issue number 10, pages 69 to 71.

everything from his superiors as God's will, should have made an exception here.

He had been ordained a priest in 1910. It usually does not take long to give a new priest the faculty of hearing confessions, but this was not the case with Padre Pio. And this time, it seemed our friar was fairly trembling with the desire to be able to dedicate himself to this ministry. Between April 1911 and April 1913, he wrote eighteen letters to his provincial, insisting on obtaining the faculty of hearing confessions. His superior feared for his physical health and was also uncertain whether Padre Pio had the necessary understanding of moral theology, since his studies had been disrupted by his health problems. So ironically, the most famous confessor of our era had to struggle and wait before obtaining the faculty of hearing confessions. And in addition, he would later have it revoked for three years.

He made up for his missed opportunities afterward, living in the confessional, right up to the morning of his death. To give an idea of this, on November 16, 1919, he wrote to his spiritual father: "I have been working for nineteen hours without a break. As I write this, it is one in the morning."

Hours and hours of confessions, which were often like hand-to-hand combat with Satan as he tried to wrest souls from his grasp. Much has been written about Padre Pio's method of administering confession (if one may speak of method), reporting episodes of conversions and of absolutions delayed or even completely denied. I will limit myself to a few remarks on the most evident characteristics and on what I saw in person.

It must be said, first, that hearing confessions put a tremendous strain on Padre Pio, not only because of the revulsion he felt for sin as an offense against God but also because his interior battles never gave him a moment's respite. Throughout his whole life, he felt like a terrible sinner, and he had a "nail sharp enough to pierce his brain and heart": the fear of not being in the grace of God.

As sure as he was in guiding souls, he was equally uncertain and fearful when it came to himself. In addition to this, he, too, a man like others, suffered under the weight of his weaknesses as soon as he became aware of them. A typical case is one he confided to Pope Benedict [XV] in 1917, when he realized one day that, exhausted on account of his efforts, "without wanting to, I become subject to acts of impatience. This is another thorn that pierces my heart."

When Padre Pio climbed the stairs to the altar, it seemed he was going up to Calvary; but also when he entered the confessional, he suffered a great deal from his unworthiness, from the fear of his incapacity. And yet it was precisely in administering confession, or above all there, that the Lord granted him a great charism, that of reading consciences.

How did he hear confessions?

"If you forgive the sins of any, they are forgiven; if you retain the sins of any, they are retained." These words reported in the Gospel of John (20:23) were firmly stamped on Padre Pio's heart, together with the understanding that he had to be a minister of divine mercy. But he knew he was able to give or not give absolution according to the dispositions of the penitent.

His confessional was not a vending machine of absolution, but a place of conversions. What he wanted was true repentance for all sins, whether mortal or venial. In this, he had a clear perception of the absolute holiness of God, of the need for souls not only to be in the state of grace but to be purified on this earth before they appear for judgment, because he knew very well how dreadful the pains of purgatory are.

I know of various cases of persons who, in confessing, would say things like "Father, I've been up to the usual mischief, the usual silliness ..." and he, refusing to play along: "Mischief? Silliness, to offend God? Get out of here!" For the time being, that was that.

His confessions were like events of proclamation and of salvation, of sorrow and of joy, of chastisement and of love. He attests in a letter from Foggia dated August 23, 1916: "You must know that I am not left with one moment free: a throng of souls thirsting for Jesus presses in upon me until I am at the point of throwing up my hands."[2]

He gave his all with the most evident certainty that the confessional is the tribunal of divine mercy but, at the same time, the place of ordeal for priestly charity. He had to tell one penitent: "Don't you see how black you are? Go put things back in order, change your ways, and then come and I will hear your confession." Father Tarcisio, who was present when this happened, was struck by the response, but Padre Pio said to him: "If only you knew what arrows pierced my heart first! But if I do not do this, many won't convert to God." He had little sayings he sometimes used: "I have begotten you in love and in suffering." "I can hit my children, but woe to anyone else who touches them! ... When I give them a slap, it's to get them climbing."

He filled the hearts of his penitents with hope and trust in divine forgiveness. He wrote: "Haven't you loved the Lord for quite some time? Don't you still love him? Don't you yearn to love him forever? Then no fear! Even granting that you may have committed all the sins of this world, Jesus repeats to you: your many sins are forgiven, because you have loved much."[3] And again: "Rest assured that God can reject everything in a creature conceived in sin that bears the indelible imprint inherited from

[2] *Letters*, vol. 1 (see ch. 1, n. 2).
[3] *Letters*, vol. 3.

Adam; but he absolutely cannot reject the sincere desire to love him."[4]

To a soul who asked him what the confessional is, he answered: "It is the throne where God's majesty is seated." One young man was crying, and Padre Pio asked him, "Why are you crying?" He answered, "Because you did not give me absolution." Padre Pio consoled him with tenderness: "My son, if that is so, I didn't deny you absolution to send you to hell, but to send you to heaven."

Cardinal Lercaro, during the Diocesan Eucharistic Congress in Trapani in 1969, commemorated Padre Pio in these words:

> The confessional was for him the source of so many interior, spiritual sufferings: his passion. Sin weighed upon him, the sin that he listened to, ascertained, and rebuked, but in order to call down upon it the mercy of God; the sin that in God's name he forgave, was a wound in his soul.... And he united his suffering with those of Christ so that his brothers' sins might be forgiven.

The thirst for souls also turned into prayer during the long nights of vigil. More than one of his fellow friars witnessed his pleas: "Jesus, Mary, have pity. O Jesus, I commend to you this soul, you must convert it, save it.... If men have to be punished,

[4] *Letters*, vol. 4.

punish me, I am content.... I offer for his sake my whole self." Padre Pio often used to say: "If only people knew how much a soul costs! Souls are not given as a gift: they are bought. You have no idea how much they cost Jesus. And now it is still with the same coin that they must be purchased." He wrote to Pope Benedict [XV] on June 3, 1919: "All the time is spent in untangling brothers from the snares of Satan. Blessed be God.... The greatest form of charity is that of snatching souls from the grasp of Satan in order to win them for Christ. And this is just what I do assiduously day and night.... There are splendid conversions."[5] To Father Pellegrino, impatient with the demanding behavior of some persons, he urges, "You must make yourself fresh bread for hungry teeth and good wine for parched throats."

And he wanted a real resolution. We often confess casually, almost out of habit. With him, this was not possible. One time I ran into a former high school classmate who was spending his vacation in San Giovanni. He said to me, "You know what? I had to go to the Padre three times for him to give me absolution. I couldn't understand why he was sending me away; I thought I was being sincere and repentant. The third time, I had made a certain decision to correct a defect of mine. I

[5] *Letters*, vol. 1.

didn't say anything, but the Padre already knew and absolved me."

This man was able to do this because he was there for a longer stay, but it was not possible for everyone [to go to confession again]. Especially during the summer months, when the crowds were largest, there was a rule in place: if someone went to confession and then wanted to go again, he had to wait at least seven days. This is why many left San Giovanni without absolution.

It is a practice worth pondering over. Many times, one of the other friars would speak to Padre Pio about it, urging him to be more lenient. But he would reply, "I do it for their good. Don't you believe that I suffer more than they do? But if you only knew how I follow them afterward, how I don't let up on them!"

I have personally known people who left San Giovanni Rotondo angry with Padre Pio because they did not receive absolution, and they determined not to set foot there again. But sooner or later, they would feel an almost irresistible desire to go back. Often they were the very ones who became the most faithful visitors to San Giovanni.

Padre Pio loved the sinner, but he was unbending when it came to the sin. He was known for his insults: "Lowlife, you're going to hell!" "When are you going to quit being such a pig?" "Don't you know that's mortal sin? Get out of here!" People could plead, insist, but it was hard to get him to change his mind. He didn't look anyone in the face: rich or poor, beautiful or ugly, he looked into their souls. All in line, all the same, whether politician or factory worker.

Many confided to me, "Here it seems like you're at the judgment seat of God, with your soul laid bare." There was also a human element that played into this: the long waits for days or even weeks and the need to keep things short because of the huge crowds meant that people came well prepared with what they were going to say. There was time to think, to review those few words again and again.

Another human element was the apprehension people could feel, in part because of the long wait that made the encounter seem even more import-ant. Padre Pio was known—and we would talk with each other about this—for being as sweet as could be when someone was truly repentant; for being an expert at getting souls to aim ever higher; for being patient, right after confession, in listening to what came next: I believe almost everyone who went to Padre Pio had something in particular to ask of him, for himself or for others.

I found that I enjoyed even the wait because, espe-cially among the men, who were never as numer-ous as the women, there arose a sort of solidarity, of reciprocal confidence. Often (perhaps even more with the priests who were waiting, but also with others) it would happen that someone would confide what he was going to say to the Padre and what his fears were.

Whenever someone came out of the confessional, a little crowd would form around him, a bit off to the side: "What did the Padre say to you? And what did you say to him?" Then there might be some advice on how to go about it next time. It seemed that after the secret confession came the public one.

The grace of God was certainly hard at work getting souls to understand the gravity of sin. One day a man confided to me, "Believe me, Father. Certain things that I have always confessed without difficulty, with him I can't bring myself to say them."

One evening, I was stopped outside the church, which was already closed, by a man who was certainly over the age of sixty. We recognized each other because we had been in the same line waiting for our turn. He said to me, "Look, Father, I didn't come here to confess. I know very well that I could go to any priest and he would absolve me. But I don't believe in it. I spent many years working in America; you have no idea of the sins I've committed. I can't believe that a whole life of sin can be forgiven all at once, just because someone goes and tells a priest about it." I replied, "Then why did you get in line for confession? What will you say to the Padre?" And he repeated almost mechanically a little speech that he had memorized and recited over and over: "I will say to him, 'Father, I didn't come here to confess. I don't believe that ...'"

The next morning I was among the first to go to confession. Afterward I waited there, and that other man's turn came. I watched carefully: a little hesitation at first; then the dialogue typical of confessions; finally, the Padre's hand raised for the slow sign of the cross in absolution. Right after leaving the confessional, the man came up to me beaming, happy. "As soon as I started my little speech: 'Father, I didn't come here', he interrupted me. 'Son, just how many have you managed to rack up over more than forty years? You know, the whole lot of them, all shapes and sizes? But remember, your sins, no matter how many and how serious they may be, are limited; God's mercy is infinite.'"

He had to stop for a moment, too emotional to go on. Then he told me that in that moment, he felt something inside him, like a voice that was saying, "If God's mercy is infinite, even if you had committed ten times as many sins, they would still all fit inside." So he broke down, confessed, and was really happy.

I think back on the gift Padre Pio had for reading consciences, for seeing what was inside them. One day, thanks to a friar who was a friend of mine, I found myself at the door of Padre Pio's cell, the famous room number 5, on which was a little sign with a saying from Saint Bernard: "Mary is the whole reason for my hope."

The Padre would be coming back in a few minutes. There was already a young man, twenty-five to thirty years old, waiting for him. No one but the two of us, with a chance to talk with Padre Pio a bit in private: it seemed like a dream to me. But none of it went as I had expected. When the Padre arrived, he said right away, "I'm sorry, I don't have time. I have to cut off my head." We didn't understand. Padre Pio nodded to me in greeting, then turned decisively to the other: "You cannot go on like this. No. You don't want to offend God, but you don't want to let go of the sin. No. You cannot move forward like this. You have to decide. No. You cannot go on like this ..." And he went into his room shaking his head.

I saw that the young man had tears in his eyes. I asked him:

"Did you understand what the Padre was trying to say to you?"

"Yes. It's my tragedy."

"Have you spoken with him before?"

"No, never. This is the first time I've been here."

"Did someone talk to the Padre about you?"

"No. No one from my family or my town knows I'm here."

"Do you want to talk about it with me?"

"No. Let me reflect."

The next morning, when Padre Pio came to the sacristy, I saw his hair was closely cropped and his beard had been trimmed. I understood what he was trying to tell us when he said he had to cut off his head: he had an appointment with the friary barber.

Sometimes, even in confession, he would display his innate sense of humor. One time I confessed that I had entertained thoughts of pride. He said to me seriously, "If these are qualities that you have, they are from the Lord, who has given them to you, and in laying claim to them, you are a thief and deserve prison. If you think you have qualities that you do not have, you are a madman and deserve the asylum. Choose, son: prison or the asylum." And he gave me a cheery smile.

Other times his responses were simple as could be. "Father, how does one truly love the Lord with all one's strength?" "Son, do not offend him." This is what the Gospel says: You love me if you do what I say.

I would like to add that his behavior was highly personalized; it could not be generalized or imitated. I remember one man who had been widowed twice and asked Padre Pio if he should remarry. Padre Pio told him the first marriage came from God, the second from man, the third from the devil. When someone else asked the same question, he gave a completely different answer.

It was the same with his strictness, above all in denying absolution. I knew a young priest who spent his summer vacation in San Giovanni every year. One year, after hearing about so many cases, he went back to his diocese and was stricter in the confessional, sometimes denying absolution. The summer after this, Padre Pio really blasted him: "Who do you think you are—Padre Pio? I know when to deny absolution. You have to absolve!" This too, clearly, was a response that applied to that case.

As a confessor, Padre Pio left an indelible impression with the gesture he made when he pronounced the words of absolution. All priests absolve, but Padre Pio's absolution left a peace that was a true gift from God—at times with a little something extra.

One of my priest friends happened to see, while Padre Pio was raising his hand, a little stream of blood dripping from the fingerless glove. It really stuck with him, this glimpse of what confessions cost Padre Pio.

7

THE MASS OF PADRE PIO

On the prayer card for his first Mass Padre Pio wrote the following:

> Jesus, my breath and my life,
> how I tremble today as I lift you up
> in a mystery of love;
> together with you, may I be for the world
> way, truth, life,
> and, through you, holy priest, perfect victim.

I attended many Masses with Padre Pio, but it's hard for me to talk about them. There was something special about his Mass, which made it the focal point for the crowds that flocked to San Giovanni. The things I can say have been seen, spoken of, and repeated by many, which means people in general consistently grasped at least certain aspects of Padre Pio's Mass.

"Do this in memory of me": it is quite clear that, in speaking of Padre Pio's Mass, one is not touching upon the essential nature of the eucharistic sacrifice, which is identical in every Mass, regardless of the priest who celebrates it. It may be more hurried or more leisurely; it may seem to be conducted with more or less devotion; the people may go more willingly to this one rather than another. We priests have often heard the recommendation "Celebrate your Mass as if it were the first of your life or as if it were the last"; other times, it is said, "Watch how a priest celebrates Mass and you will already have a sense of who he is."

These may seem to be superficial observations, but in reality they contain something true, profound. The essential nature of the Mass is always the same, because the primary priest is Christ; but the priest also brings something of his own, sometimes a great deal. It is just like those who attend: there are many ways of attending the divine sacrifice—from those who show up only so that they can say, "I've been to Mass," to those who participate with all their faculties, even to those who offer themselves in union with the divine victim.

The Mass, celebrated or attended, can also be a mirror of our relationship with Jesus, of our love for him, our understanding, intimacy, dedication.

These are concepts that can help us, that can show us the dispositions we need in order to get even a glimpse of what Padre Pio's Mass was, this celebration into which the Padre put his whole self and expressed his whole self: his love for God Crucified, for the God who is Love, for the God who is Victim for sins, for the God who is Savior, for the God who made him a participant in his work of redemption.

We should think back over Padre Pio's entire life: over his long—I would say uninterrupted—meditations on the Passion of Christ, accompanied by many tears; over his horror for sin, his love for Jesus, the offering of his whole self as a victim for sinners, for the souls in purgatory, for the Church and the world. And we should keep in mind how the Lord chose to associate this minister of his with the work of redemption: the struggles against Satan, the dark night of faith, the growing participation in the Passion, culminating in the visible stigmata.

So it should come as no surprise that when Padre Pio celebrated Mass, it truly looked as if he was reliving the Passion of Christ. When he went up to the altar, with those pained steps of his, it really seemed that he was going up to Calvary. The people made the responses out loud, which was rather rare back then, when the altar boys were usually the only ones to respond. This, too, showed the efforts of those present to participate as much as they could.

Everyone's eyes were fixed on that face and its evident contortions of suffering, although equally evident were the Padre's efforts to try to keep them from showing. Tears would often stream down his face, and he would wipe them with a handkerchief that he always kept within reach, many times making it look as if he were wiping off sweat. Then there was the striking of his breast at the *mea culpa* and at the Agnus Dei, with blows so hard it was a mystery how he could do it with his wounded hands; the prolonged kneeling that sometimes gave the impression that he did not have the strength to get up; and the long pauses, with his eyes staring and shrouded with tears, when it seemed as if he couldn't go on anymore.

Some have called Padre Pio's Mass "an authentic supernatural spectacle". There was certainly nothing theatrical about it. But why did people come from all over the world, to such an uncomfortable place and at such an unusual hour, to attend that never-ending Mass? And when it did come to an end, why would they want it to last even longer? There is no doubt that Padre Pio was reliving the Passion of Jesus.

We know of saints, often stigmatized, who, on Fridays or during Holy Week, relived the Passion. I think of Saint Veronica Giuliani, Saint Gemma Galgani, Therese Neumann, Venerable Alexandrina Maria Da Costa ... But no one lived it during the Mass.

Padre Pio is so far the only stigmatized priest. And this reliving the Passion as a priest during the

Mass seems to me to have had a particular aim that the faithful, perhaps unconsciously, intuited.

There was no special mystery in the Mass of Padre Pio; the true mystery, of which we understand so little, is *the Mass*! It is a sacrifice; it is the unbloody memorial of the Cross; it is the immolation of Jesus, who offers himself to the Father as a victim for us and gives himself to us as the food of eternal life. We try to help ourselves with expressions that are true, but they are incomplete.

It seems to me that the people, in observing Padre Pio, were really making an effort to understand the true meaning of the Mass. Many, priests and faithful, have told me they came to understand what the Mass is only after attending the Masses of Padre Pio.

Asked to explain the Holy Mass, he replied, "My children, how can I explain it to you? The Mass is infinite, like Jesus." And he added, "The world could go on even without the sun, but it could not go on without the Holy Mass."

As for what happened in souls during those Masses, that was entirely and solely the work of the Holy Spirit: people who had come out of curiosity, crying like children; men who did not believe, and during that sacrifice felt all their doubts disappear; so many who were hardened against repentance, hardened against forgiveness, hardened against changing their ways, and during that Mass formed the firm resolution to make that change; many young men and women who, during that sacrifice, saw all of their uncertainties crumble and gave themselves entirely to God, in the priestly or religious life.

There was one man I knew, set in his ways, who never went to church anymore. I was stunned when he confided to me that he had spent several days in San Giovanni and had gone to the Padre's Mass every morning. I asked him what he had felt, and I have never forgotten what he said: "I always stayed in the back of the church, ashamed of myself; every now and then I would look up from the floor at the Padre. I was amazed that he would tolerate my presence and did not kick me out." He seemed to me like the publican in the Gospel, the one Jesus says went away forgiven.

One bishop told me, with great conviction, "It doesn't take anything else to understand who Padre Pio is; all that is needed is to attend his Mass."

Every Mass was an agony for Padre Pio. But the graces came down like rain, and often they were extraordinary. There was no need for explanation: it was clear that this was a sacrifice, the sacrifice of Jesus, to which was united the sacrifice of the celebrant, with those present striving to take part in it also.

I know very well that many have written more and better than I have about Padre Pio's Mass. But I think it is always helpful to consider it, especially for the faithful who so easily neglect the Mass or become distracted when they attend; helpful also for the priests who sometimes rush through it as fast as they can.

But do they know what the Mass is?

8

AN ENORMOUS FAMILY

Further on, we will take a look at one of Padre Pio's visible initiatives, the Home for the Relief of Suffering. But before this comes one of his great works, built not out of bricks but out of human hearts: the spiritual children of Padre Pio.

It is not easy to establish a starting date; every priest has spiritual children from the time there are persons who consistently avail themselves of his priestly ministry. With Padre Pio, it is not enough to speak of consistency; I think it is more precise to speak of stability. And this was a matter not only of stability in appealing to him but sometimes even of physical stability, of residence.

I have already noted, as the first core group, those persons who were going to him as a confessor and spiritual guide back in 1917. He often accompanied and advised them by letter when they lived far away. This is how we have come to possess that valuable heritage that is the correspondence of Padre Pio.

Undoubtedly there were persons so struck by the impact Padre Pio had on them as to want to visit him frequently or even move nearby. Anyone familiar with the circle that formed around the Padre knew who *l'americana* was: Mary Pyle, who already in 1925 had become aware of Padre Pio's holiness and, in order to be close to him, had built a house just down the hill from the friary, where she would spend the rest of her life.

Exaggeration? Fanaticism? It seemed that way to some at first. But if we think back, for example, on the origin of cenobitic life, when so many left everything to build huts near one who was esteemed a true man of God and to dedicate themselves to a life of prayer under his spiritual guidance, we see that Mary Pyle's decision was not so unusual.

I should add that the *americana* did a lot of good for those around her. She was very hospitable, so much so that Padre Pio's mom and dad stayed with her and died in her home.

How did someone become one of Padre Pio's spiritual children? Simply by going to him regularly for confession. But there was also another system, employed above all by those who could not go to see him often. When I learned of it, this was the way I used. All it took was to ask him, to request to be accepted as one of his spiritual children. As far as I know, he said yes to everyone. As he himself stated a number of times, "I don't call anyone, and I don't turn anyone away."

In time, I got the idea for an even better system. After I became a priest, I, too, began to have my spiritual children. What could I do to be more helpful to them? I talked about my problem with Padre Pio and made a special request: "I ask you to accept as your spiritual children all of mine, present and future." After a few moments of reflection, Padre Pio accepted, quite firmly. Then I said, "Just think, now mine will be calling you *Grandpa Pio!*" He had a good laugh at that one.

I can say Padre Pio was true to his word. To all of them he is Padre (never Grandpa!); but many times, he has helped my spiritual children in extraordinary ways, even if they were not thinking about him or aware of our agreement at all. For my part, I must say that Padre Pio's help is extremely effective and sometimes palpable, especially since I dedicated myself to the ministry of exorcism.

Of course, Padre Pio was particularly demanding with his children; he brought them up for effort, for duty, for the cross, even for heroism when he saw that they were capable of it. And there is no doubt he had great charisms for this purpose as well. The episodes are countless.

In San Giovanni, I met a young man who told me about what had happened to him. Others may

have heard about this, and it seems to me someone has written about it, but I got the story firsthand.
He had resolved, as a means of overcoming his human
respect, to make a nice, big sign of the cross every
time he passed a church. For a while, things went just
fine. But one day, he was out with two friends, the
kind who have nothing to do with the faith. They
were passing in front of a church. "Do I cross myself?
Do I not cross myself? Am I giving a good example
or setting myself up as a joke?" Needless to say, while
the young man was still trying to decide, they passed
right by the door of the church. Then he heard a
well-known voice at his ear: "Coward!"

As soon as he could, he went to see Padre Pio.
Right away when he saw him, the Padre burst out
laughing. Then he became serious and said, "That's
all you got this time, but if you do it again, you'll be
feeling a smack."

One of my fellow Paulines, Father Francesco
Testi, was particularly dear to me. We were both
from Modena, had known each other since our col-
lege days, and had been through the war together.
He was the son of Mama Nina, who was well
known throughout the whole province of Modena,
as was his uncle, Father Zeno Saltini. He often went
to see Padre Pio and sometimes stayed for quite a
while, so the Padre knew him well. When he was
ordained a priest in 1952, he celebrated his first Mass
at his mother's chapel, part of the pious association

she had founded. The following day, he celebrated in Motta di Cavezzo, at a little chapel where there was a very kindly old nun, Sister Erminia. At a certain point in the celebration, the nun began to clap her hands, she was so delighted. After the Mass was finished, she was asked why she had done that, and she candidly replied, "Because Padre Pio was there. Didn't you see him?" Also present was Mr. Cremonini, one of Padre Pio's most faithful devotees. That same evening, he departed for San Giovanni Rotondo, and the next morning he approached the friar: "Padre, yesterday Father Francesco Testi celebrated his first Mass in Motta." And Padre Pio replied: "I know. I was there too!"

The prayer groups

It is important to remember something else that began to happen spontaneously. The spiritual children of Padre Pio who lived in the same city, or close enough, started to meet together. They would talk about Padre Pio and about their experiences with him, but above all they would pray. And after the first few meetings, they limited themselves to prayer alone.

This is how the first prayer groups came about, even before Padre Pio expressly encouraged these—or at least they were the seeds of the future prayer groups.

It was the groups of spiritual children who enlivened the special milestones of Padre Pio's life, even when the conditions were unfavorable on account of the two harrowing decades through which the Padre's life would pass. These milestones would have gone by in silence if they had not been marked by the ever-growing ranks of children gathering around their father. The first of these dates was August 10, 1935, the silver anniversary of Padre Pio's priestly ordination. This was right in the middle of one of the two dark periods. Every special feature had been prohibited: the sung Mass, the kissing of the hand, the singing of the Te Deum, all of which were customary on such an occasion. But the little church was packed with faithful. The same thing happened again on January 22, 1953, the fiftieth anniversary of the Padre's religious vows. This was during the second black decade. All that was allowed was a little commemorative holy card, with words that had been dictated by Padre Pio, beginning, "Fifty years of religious life, fifty years fastened to the cross". To make up for this, a large group of his spiritual children was present.

The prayer groups got a solid push from the words of the pope. Pius XII, especially from 1947 on, insisted on the need for prayer. Padre Pio felt he had to respond to the pope's appeals and, in 1948 and 1949, decisively encouraged the formation of these groups, which on September 12, 1959, in conjunction with the National Eucharistic Congress, held their first national convention in Catania.

The next day, September 13, the consecration of Italy to the Immaculate Heart of Mary was finally pronounced. This event was broadcast live on radio and television, followed by the radio message of John XXIII. I emphasize these events, in which I took part, because Padre Pio's prayer groups made an enormous contribution to them with their prayers; I received testimony of this when I was given a collection of archived material from these groups, which I later handed on to the Tempio Nazionale a Madre Maria in Trieste, built in commemoration of the event.

On May 5, 1966, there was a twofold occasion: the ten-year anniversary of the inauguration of the Home for the Relief of Suffering and the second international convention of the prayer groups. Padre Pio spoke to the "groups now spread all over the world" and urged them, "Let us gather periodically for prayer in common. The present society does not pray; that is why it is going to pieces."

During the last days of his life, Padre Pio had the satisfaction of hearing Paul VI give formal recognition to his prayer groups.

Other milestones in the Padre's life were enlivened by his spiritual children, in spite of the unjust onslaughts that were unleashed against him. August 10, 1960, was another eagerly anticipated day, the golden anniversary of Padre Pio's priestly ordination.

In the big new church, filled with around seven thousand faithful, his Mass was attended by three bishops and by the highest authorities of the province and of the town. There was even a joyful torchlight procession in the evening.

Finally a fitting celebration! Messages of congratulations came from statesmen, cardinals, and bishops, including one letter of good wishes from the cardinal of Milan, the future Paul VI.

Better than a fax

How did so many children manage to communicate with Padre Pio? There were the usual methods: going to confession or being received in the parlor (for those who had important matters to discuss and were already acquaintances), saying something in passing, writing to him, having a friar or another close acquaintance talk to him ...

But there was another method that many used, including myself, a method faster than the telegram or the modern-day fax, which did not exist back then: recourse to one's guardian angel. This topic alone deserves separate treatment, and, in fact, books have been written about it. It is a fact that when it was not possible to approach the Padre, either because of distance or because of the crowd, many turned with faith to Padre Pio's guardian angel or to their own guardian angels, and the messages got there right away.

I will recount just one episode no one else knows about. Vittoria Brenna, a spiritual daughter of Padre Pio and the wife of Angelo Battisti, of whom we will speak in connection with the Home for the Relief of Suffering, had a Capuchin confessor in Rome, Father Pio of Mondregañez, from Spain. He had his heart set on going to see Padre Pio but had never been given permission. Then his ministry took him to Cosenza for a while. Before going back to Rome, he prayed this prayer: "If it is true that our guardian angel knows Padre Pio and takes our messages to him, let mine tell him that since I am in the south of Italy, I would like to go see him." That same day, the superior of the Cosenza friary asked him, "Before going back to Rome, do you want to go to San Giovanni Rotondo?" He accepted enthusiastically and was on his way the very next day. At the end of his meeting with Padre Pio, he asked him, "Padre, has my guardian angel ever come to you?" And Padre Pio: "Yes, he came once, from Cosenza."

I believe that Padre Pio's mission was to be for us a living reminder of all the mysteries of the faith: the redemptive Passion of the Lord and his mercy; the existence of heaven, hell, and purgatory; and also the existence of the angels, and of our guardian angels in particular, who tend to us twenty-four hours a day with astonishing care and about whom we perhaps never think.

9

THE FIRST DECADE OF FIRE

1923–1933

Too often we forget that where there are human creatures, there are also human defects. One of these defects is fanaticism. We encounter this continually around persons who stir up enthusiasm for the most varied reasons. We find it around Jesus and many saints; we encounter it with actors and politicians, singers and sports figures. One cannot kill a man because he has defects; one cannot put down a movement because it contains some disordered elements. It is even worse when punishing the extremists means harming the innocent. There is the conviction that the evil is being pulled up by the roots, when what is happening instead is what Jesus applies to himself: "I will strike the shepherd, and the sheep of the flock will be scattered" (Mt 26:31).

Was there an attempt to destroy Padre Pio? Let's let the facts speak for themselves. Measures were already being taken in June 1922, when Padre Pio was barred from all contact with his spiritual father, Father Benedetto, in person and in writing. We should recognize that Father Benedetto was for twelve years, from 1910 to 1922, an excellent spiritual director, wise and prudent. To this day, it is hard to understand the reasons for that provision, which seems completely unjustified. Father Benedetto always had the greatest trust in his superiors and confreres. It is clear this was nothing but an attempt to strike a blow against Padre Pio, by depriving him of a source of support and a valuable guide.

But then the measures against the Padre became increasingly burdensome. On May 31, 1923, the Holy Office declared it had carried out an investigation of occurrences attributed to Padre Pio (What were these? No one has ever found out), concluding that "no evidence was found that these were supernatural." But then came the main event, the result that was being sought no matter what the cost. The order came that Padre Pio was to be transferred, and he was prohibited from celebrating Mass in public. What erupted was almost a popular uprising: many times the sensibility of the people sees matters rather more clearly than the religious authorities do.

In accord with the civil authorities, the friary was put under surveillance around the clock, to prevent the Padre from being transferred. The mayor convinced the provincial of the Capuchins to rescind the measures; on June 26, his superiors urged the ever-obedient Padre Pio to celebrate Mass in public once again.

Meanwhile word got out that the superior general of the friars had decided to send Padre Pio to an isolated friary in Marche; he had urged prudence and firmness but had not set a date. This measure was later suspended. In exchange, the Holy Office, on July 24, 1924, exhorted the faithful to abstain completely from going to see Padre Pio and from writing to him.

Who knows what crimes Padre Pio was committing in the Church of Santa Maria delle Grazie and what spiritual harm was being caused by his letters! But that was the order.

There was more to come. On April 23, 1926, the Holy Office declared Giorgio Berlutti's book about Padre Pio [authored by Emanuele Brunatto] "prohibited" and declared it "a duty of the faithful not to go see Padre Pio".

On July 11, 1926, the Holy Office pronounced the same sentence against the book by Giuseppe Cavaciocchi and repeated the same warning to the faithful: don't go to Padre Pio! On May 22, 1931, the Holy Office pronounced the same sentence for the book by Alberto Del Fante and repeated the warning to the faithful: no visits and no letters.

This brings us to the tragedy of May 31, 1931, when Padre Pio was stripped of his faculties: he was prohibited from celebrating in public but allowed to celebrate in private, inside the friary; and above all, he was forbidden to hear confessions.

When, a few days later, Father Raffaele was assigned the painful task of communicating the decree of the Holy Office to him, Padre Pio simply replied, "May God's will be done." For more than two years, he lived like a prisoner (this was his impression)—years of great prayer and great suffering. To the friars who tried to speak a word of comfort to him, he replied, "It is for souls that I feel the suffering of this trial."

Harrowing years, with no telling how long this severe punishment would last and no telling what the reasons were. He had not been accused of anything, and no one had given him the chance to exonerate himself or to tell his side of the story.

And yet he still had the strength to be cheerful with his fellow friars, to keep from burdening them with his cross. He felt "as if in prison" but offered everything to God, sustained by the conviction that even this was part of his "great mission".

Meanwhile, outside the storm was raging. The press was certainly not keeping quiet, much less the people. There had to be reasons, and if these were not known, there were always those who were able to make them up. There was talk of accusations concerning the donations that were given or sent to him, which he promptly turned over to the superior, also indicating the intention of the donor. There was even talk that women were going to the church at night, and who knew what was happening in there? Then there was an avalanche of anonymous letters. Needless to say, even apart from the rumors, there was great popular discontent, so much so that the *podestà* [the Fascist-era equivalent of a mayor in Italy] asked the regional prefect to intervene with the Holy See.

It is difficult to pin down the causes of these events, especially if one wants to avoid creating controversy. In this book, I am striving to keep from doing so, because my aim is to bring the person of Padre Pio to light; I have no interest in others. But I still have to say something to illustrate the proceedings. It is well known that the information that came from Manfredonia archbishop Pasquale Gagliardi was bad, but for the sake of charity, I prefer not to speak of this bishop.

There is no doubt that Pius XI was greatly influenced by the bluntly negative views of Father [Agostino] Gemelli, whom he greatly admired. This aspect certainly played a key role, and even the Holy Office acted on the basis of information he had, but also in obedience to the instructions it received.

I would like to give some attention to the attitude of Father Gemelli. This is, in part, because I knew him; he had a convert's forceful personality and left a profound impression with the foundation

of his Catholic University of the Sacred Heart, his
secular institutes, his studies. I also owe him a personal debt of gratitude for the regard that led him to
put me on the pastoral staff of his university.

Cardinal [Giacomo] Antonelli, who knew him
very well, once made a great point to me: "Father
Gemelli has defects so obvious they can be seen a
mile away, but he loves Jesus Christ so much that
all is forgiven." It is only in the light of his unique
character that one can understand his stubborn bias
against Padre Pio and his insistence that he had ana-
lyzed the stigmata when in fact he never saw them,
since he never got the necessary authorization for
this from the Holy Office.

In Father Gemelli, heroic virtues grew alongside
substantial defects, due to his natural temperament;
he tried to correct these when he became aware
of them and to the extent that he was able to. I
will be glad indeed if he is elevated to the glory of
the saints: it will show cantankerous types that they,
too, can attain holiness.

Rehabilitation

Padre Pio may never have known why they con-
demned him and why they absolved and rehabil-
itated him, just as he may never have understood
the human motives that kept him in San Giovanni
Rotondo in spite of all the orders for his transfer.

For his part, he accepted every provision from the hands of God and never tired of repeating that, for him, the will of his superiors expressed the divine will. His personal serenity and spirit of obedience were in stark contrast with the storm that was being stirred up outside the friary, by resentful minds or by spirits gone bad.

Already at the beginning of what I have called "the first decade of fire", as we have seen, there was talk of transferring Padre Pio from San Giovanni Rotondo. On July 30, 1923, the superior general of the Capuchins had drawn up the written order for the transfer. Father Luigi, who was given the thankless task of communicating this order to the Padre, received an entirely forthright reply: "Here I am, at your orders. Let's go right now." But it was midnight, and apart from the fact that the transfer did not set a date, the superior general had reserved for himself the duty of establishing when the order should be carried out. This latter communication never came, and instead, the other measures we have already considered went into effect.

What brought about the rehabilitation of Padre Pio? A number of elements were probably working together. The most important of these was the initiative of several Capuchin bishops who evidently held their confrere in high esteem and wanted to get to the bottom of these sanctions. The most persistent were Treviso bishop [Blessed] Andrea

Giacinto Longhin and Cornelio Sebastiano Cucca-
rollo, bishop of Bovino.

This latter, since he was stationed close to San
Giovanni (Bovino is also in the province of Foggia),
was charged with ascertaining the truth of the accusations leveled against Padre Pio. He carried out his
task very meticulously, and his conclusions were so
clear that he reported them directly to Pius XI. The
pope became convinced that the accusations were
baseless and revoked the prohibitions on Mass in
public and on confession.

Also in the plus column for Padre Pio were the
results of the investigation ordered by the Holy
Father, who was evidently harboring doubts. This
had been led by Luca Ermenegildo Pasetto, bishop
of Gera, with the assistance of Monsignor Felice
Bevilacqua. No less active was Father Orione, an
admirer of Padre Pio, who had a firm grasp of the
facts and influence with eminent churchmen.

I am less certain when it comes to the significance of contributions from other persons, Emanuele Brunatto in particular, who were scandalized by
the unjust treatment of which Padre Pio had been
victim and tried to intervene forcefully, threatening
to create scandal in the press. I prefer not to get into
this subject so as to avoid controversy.

What I am bound to mention, however, is Padre
Pio's response to these efforts: he did all he could to
oppose them, made it clear that he was completely

against them, and begged that such means be abandoned in favor of trust in the Lord and his instruments, the ecclesiastical authorities.

In the meantime, another change had taken place that was to prove providential on many occasions. In late 1931, Archbishop Andrea Cesarano had been appointed head of the diocese of Manfredonia, where he would provide excellent leadership until 1967. Meanwhile, thanks to Pius XI, Padre Pio was getting his faculties back, albeit more gradually than the faithful would have liked: on July 16, 1933, he was finally let out of the "prison" he had been in since June 11, 1931, and went back to saying Mass in church; on March 25, 1934, he was allowed to hear men's confessions, and on May 12, those of women. After three years!

I will leave to the imagination how overjoyed the people of San Giovanni were and how the faithful again started streaming in from all over the world. The Padre went back to his old routine as if nothing had happened: altar and confessional, in addition to a great deal of prayer. He ate and slept very little; the other friars never understood where he found the strength. And yet he seemed tireless, and the influx of people was so great that, starting on January 7, 1950, a reservation system had to be set up.

A HOME FOR THOSE
WHO SUFFER

Inherent in Christianity is a special sensitivity toward all the sufferings of one's brothers, in particular those of the sick. Just think of the healings that Jesus performed and of the reward he promised: "I was sick and you visited me"; think of the foundation of the hospitaller orders and the building of hospitals, almost all of which began as pious foundations.

In terms of Padre Pio's sensitive spirit, I would say there were two powerful factors that fostered this sensibility in his heart, which was already so open to every need of his brothers. There was his personal experience, and there was his continual contact with persons who, directly or by mail, told him about their troubles and asked for help. Added to this was the desolate situation of the territory surrounding the Padre, a vast area devoid of medical care, from the lowland swamps to the rocky slopes of Mount Gargano.

We can say Padre Pio was always ill. Because he was sickly since his childhood, his studies were repeatedly interrupted by health problems; we have seen that he was forced to spend seven years outside the friary, in Pietrelcina, and we have made note of those high fevers of his that drove the doctors crazy and got him dismissed from military service.

The high fever caused him acute suffering, many times keeping him stuck in bed, unable even to celebrate Mass. Coughs, stomach cramps, arthritis, and maladies his doctors couldn't explain afflicted him for practically his whole life. The problems intensified during his last decade, when he would be completely exhausted by the evening, always ready to welcome "sister death".

In his last years, he had to drag himself along when he walked; it was truly painful to watch him climb the stairs. From March of 1968 on, he had to use a wheelchair to get around.

Sorely tried by his own suffering in the flesh, he was very sensitive to the illnesses of others, which besieged him almost continually; these were recounted to him in the confessional, in the church, in the hallways, in brief meetings, or through the letters that piled up. It had become almost an unspoken rule that when there was nothing more to be done for a sick person, it was time to turn to Padre Pio.

I remember that we did this for my father as well, when the doctors had given up hope. The Padre had so much compassion for the sick that he would have liked to take upon himself all of their ills. But this is not possible, just as it is not possible to remove suffering from mankind. But it is possible to give relief.

This possibility, of giving relief to the sick and of bringing aid to that area so barren of medical care, was already on Padre Pio's mind in 1922, encouraged in part by the donations he received with the earmark, "For doing good". But it was in 1940 that his first vague desires took on definitive and concrete form. At this point, it is necessary to recall three of his spiritual children who played a big part in implementing Padre Pio's plans. The affection that bound them to the Padre was such that they were already living permanently nearby. They are the pharmacist Carlo Kisvarday, from Zadar; the physician Guglielmo Sanguinetti, from Parma; and the agronomist Mario Sanvico, from Perugia. They immediately became the main advisers and architects of the huge project.

On January 9, 1940, Padre Pio firmly took the initiative. He called those stalwart sons around him and told them clearly that a great earthly work was going to begin that very evening and would go on and develop after his death. Something had to be done for the sick of the Gargano region, and not only for them. He assured them that there, beside the little church of Graces [Santa Maria delle Grazie], a large hospital would arise.

As soon as the news of Padre Pio's decision got out, donations began pouring in from all over: from small donations comparable to the widow's mite to the lavish donations of those with extensive financial means. The enthusiasm was such that some were immediately on edge: the fear was that this would be a flash in the pan, that it could all come to an abrupt halt. Instead, it became a constant resource that made it possible to carry out that seemingly impossible project.

I think back on the hillside to the right of the church that I used to climb like a chamois to contemplate the panorama from above. It is true that I loved to go up the steepest part, near the church, where the monument to Padre Pio and the broad staircase leading up to the Via Crucis now stand. But it made no sense to me, looking out toward the town, how enough of that rocky slope could be flattened to make room for a grandiose hospital complex.

Padre Pio really liked to do things on a large scale, with foresight that could not have come from a poor kid from Pietrelcina. He had never seen such an undertaking on this earth; it is likely enough that the Lord had shown it to him in a vision.

In 1946, the company that would oversee the enterprise was formed. What name should be given to it and to the new building? Padre Pio had no hesitation: the Home for the Relief of Suffering. He did not want it spoken of as a hospital or a clinic; a *home*, a family term that recalls the domestic hearth. And the purpose: to give relief to those who suffer, a relief directed first to souls and then to bodies. It was indeed a work of God and of human charity, having arisen thanks to the donations that came in from all over the world.

Since it was a work of God and the fruit of charity, Padre Pio wanted it to be an instrument for transmitting God's love to the sick and to those who would come to that home for surgery. And who should be given preference, if one can speak of preference for persons who have suffering in common? Here, too, Padre Pio was clear: "This home is first of all for the sick who are poor." But he wanted everyone to be treated equally, with fraternal charity.

Too often the sick person in the hospital feels more like a thing than a person; he feels like a number. No longer Mr. X or Mrs. Y, but bed number 32. Not here; here the sick person was supposed to feel like a brother being cared for by brothers.

There was a period during which I visited the Home quite a bit. These were the years when—in addition, of course, to my main desire, to see Padre Pio—I had various friends among the friars. These included the superior, Father Carmelo, but even more so Father Mariano and an old friar of the province of Salerno, Father Clemente, with childlike sky-blue eyes. One day I said to him, "It's good to be here with all of you." He simply replied, "What else do you expect where God's grace is found?" I was also friends with a surgeon from the region of Emilia-Romagna who had left the hospital in his city to live and work there in San Giovanni. I asked him if he had ever run into trouble in carrying out his delicate profession. He replied, "No! Here, if I'm not sure what to do, to operate or not, I ask Padre Pio, and he always gives me the solution!"

But I've gotten ahead of myself. In 1947, the first stone of the new building was laid. It seemed like madness, and instead it was a miracle of charity and pluck. I would be remiss not to recall two other architects of the project, whom I knew personally: the engineer Luigi Ghisleri, who designed the first majestic edifice with its distinctive columns on the facade that bring to mind something sacred, like a cathedral. I also think back on the tireless builder Angelo Lupi and his infinite inventiveness in the face of any sort of difficulty.

Angelo Lupi reminds me of another Angelo, Angelo Battisti, who held a position of great responsibility at the Vatican Secretariat of State and in 1957 was appointed by Padre Pio to act as his attorney. He was the first president and the first administrator of the Home. I had the chance to meet him toward the end of his life, when he was afflicted with a very unusual cross in purification of his holy life. We can really say in this case as well, just as with Padre Pio, that the Lord made use of the devil in order to sanctify a soul: he, in fact, suffered a long diabolical possession.

On May 5, 1956, just ten years after it was begun, the Home saw its solemn inauguration. It seemed impossible that the rocky hillside, truly desolate to look at and offering such a bleak view of its surroundings, should now present such an enchantingly beautiful edifice. Other builders were later added to the first, and new units joined those planned from the start.

With its cutting-edge equipment it became one of the best hospitals in Europe, without losing its character as a fraternal and welcoming *home*. In expanding its services for those in need, it has now opened a nursing home.

Thirty years have gone by since the death of Padre Pio, but the extensions and improvements have never stopped.

Was this incredible success a triumph for Padre Pio? We can say that the realization of this grandiose project came about during years of tremendous martyrdom; it came to fruition precisely during that second black decade, which, as painful as this may be, has to be examined.

It is not for nothing that Saint Paul wrote to Timothy, "All who desire to live a godly life in Christ Jesus will be persecuted" (2 Tim 3:12).

Many monuments have already been raised in honor of Padre Pio, in Italy and abroad; even more will be raised in the future. But I believe his true monument is the Home for the Relief of Suffering. It is a monument born of charity and built with charity. Padre Pio was right in consistently referring to it as a "work of divine providence".

Pius XII demonstrated a keen intuition of its profound meaning when he stated on May 8, 1956, "Casa Sollievo [is] called to introduce into the care for the sick a conception that is more deeply human and at the same time more supernatural", going on to say the Home is "the fruit of one of the highest intuitions, of an ideal ripened and perfected over time and in contact with the most varied and cruel aspects of mankind's moral and physical suffering."

There is no doubt that the Home, even from an aesthetic point of view, turned out to be a true masterpiece, something that was impossible to imagine before, looking at that rocky and barren hillside. It seemed like madness when the work was begun. Now it is called a miracle. It certainly gave a new face to the entire area. Not a desolate slope anymore, but a majestic monument in the delicate pale pink of its facade of Trani marble. And Dr. Sanguinetti had a truly brilliant idea when he decided to surround the building with ten thousand trees, mostly pine, arranged with good taste. The reader can understand quite well how the current beauty of the Home and its ornamentation should make the surroundings unrecognizable for someone who had seen them before.

11

THE SECOND DECADE OF FIRE

1952–1962

I have no grudge against the Holy Office, but the reality is that, whether on account of information it had or orders it received, the flak that flew at Padre Pio always came from there. On March 11 and April 8 of 1952, the Holy Office reported to the superior general of the Capuchins quite a few problems that had been observed in San Giovanni Rotondo. On July 30 of the same year, a decree from the Holy Office banned eight books on Padre Pio. In May and then repeatedly over the following years, the members of religious orders were prohibited from circulating writings about the Padre or images of him, and organized pilgrimages to San Giovanni were banned.

I recall that, during those years, various Capuchin friends of mine, in different parts of Italy, told me they were forbidden to go see Padre Pio; even with the diocesan authorities, if a parish priest was renting a bus for a trip to visit Padre Pio, he would be met with disdain or even a direct reprimand.

We should add that, from 1952 to 1963, there was a rapid succession of superiors at the friary and in the province of Foggia, together with the transfer of friars from one province to another. All of these were reshufflings imposed by the authorities, which saddened Padre Pio even if they did not affect him directly. Then the measures against him began.

In 1954, he was prohibited from dealing with questions that arose among the staff members of the Home; anyone who knows how close that Home was to his heart can imagine the Padre's suffering at being banned from handling these matters.

In 1960, with no reason given, he was ordered to stop receiving women outside the confessional. What accusations against the old friar were lurking behind such a drastic prohibition? He could no longer go to the sacristy to hear the confession of that spiritual daughter who was so elderly and almost completely deaf!

In the same year, there began the disastrous apostolic visitation (ordered by Pope John XXIII) by Monsignor Carlo Maccari. No wonder the sculptor Messina, on the fifth station of the beautiful Via Crucis that he volunteered to carve, substituted Padre Pio's face for that of Simon of Cyrene.

It is true that the fervent atmosphere also contained elements of fanaticism; I have already talked

about this. It is true that there was some disorder
when the people were making their reservations
for confession. And when the church was opened,
there was an indecorous race for the best spots, closest to the altar. The crowds coming to San Giovanni
had become huge; the Capuchins did the best they
could and did not hesitate to eject people who were
being too aggressive or other elements who, under
the pretext of helping with crowd control, were
making the confusion even worse. Padre Pio himself often had to raise his voice.

Many times even before this, when he was coming
out of the sacristy vested for Mass, the people would
press in on him to take his hands and kiss them; he
would try to shield himself, defending himself with
his elbows. Or a buzz would go through the church
when he appeared, and he would shout ("Silence!
On your knees!") to reestablish order. I remember
one anecdote that was recounted to me by a Capuchin friend of mine, Father Michelangelo, still sought
after as a preacher in spite of his advanced age. He
was a close friend of Padre Pio and talked with him in
complete confidence. One day he said to the Padre,
"But does that seem pleasant to you, to begin Mass
angry, with that shouting?" And Padre Pio answered:
"Who's getting angry? I've never gotten angry. I just
do that to get them to be quiet."

There was another serious incident during that
period that aggravated the situation. The years 1955

to 1958 saw the downfall of the banker Giambattista Giuffrè, with whom the Capuchins of many houses, and even Padua bishop Bortignon, had deposited millions. It was also known that Padre Pio was receiving donations in abundance for building the Home for the Relief of Suffering. The temptation was very strong to redirect those funds to cover the shortfall caused by the banker's collapse.

But Padre Pio wouldn't budge: the money that was donated had to be used according to the intentions of the donors. Just as adamant were the other priests who received donations on behalf of Padre Pio, at the cost of being hit with canonical sanctions.

But as a matter of fact, these events also contributed to creating confusion and arousing suspicions that the money sent to Padre Pio was not reaching the intended destination.

Disciplinary sanctions

Suspicions led to actions, and in the most odious and indecent manner. There have been unjust measures taken against religious and priests, but the plan with Padre Pio was to monitor his private conversations. Microphones were placed in the parlor where he received visitors and, it was suspected, even in the confessional. This is one of the facts that two journalists, [Francobaldo] Chiocci and [Luciano] Cirri, documented in a three-volume work titled *Padre*

Pio, storia di una vittima, in which they go so far as to
accuse the Holy Office of ordering the placement
of those microphones. And the volumes present
transcriptions of confessions, with statements written out by the persons involved: "We declare that
we said these things to Padre Pio in confession, and
only in confession." But these very serious accusations were denied.

And it is certain that Padre Pio himself, while
speaking with one of his spiritual children, realized
that a microphone had been hidden in the parlor
and exclaimed, "So they've stooped even to this!"
If, during the first decade of fire, he felt as if he
were in prison for three years, suspended from that
ministry that was his mission, this time he felt spied
on, like the lowest of criminals.

I would like to dwell for a bit on such a grave
matter, in part because I have spoken about it with
Chiocci, the well-known journalist; not with Cirri,
who has passed away. I am sorry to say this sad affair
involved another dear friend of mine, Monsignor
Umberto Terenzi, so praiseworthy for the jump-
start he gave to the Roman shrine of [Our Lady
of] Divine Love. But this was how Monsignor
Umberto was: if his superiors gave him a task, his
obedience was total. I would say he was behind the
times. We religious used to be under a vow that was
spoken of as *blind obedience*, whereas now the Vatican II document concerning religious speaks of *active*

and responsible obedience. As for the microphones, I do not think it is possible that any were put in the confessional. They were put in the parlor; this is certain. But when Padre Pio's spiritual children went to speak with him, they sometimes took advantage of the opportunity to ask him to hear their confessions.

As if this were not enough, more suspicions and accusations were added. For example, the rumor went around that it was not clear who had ultimately gotten hold of the letters—a real mountain of them—that were addressed to Padre Pio, sometimes at the friary, other times at the Home for the Relief of Suffering, and often contained donations. Everything seemed to point toward an attack by Satan against the great work of the Home; it may have been an attempt to delay the project or even make it all go up in smoke.

The fact remains that the measures ordered by the apostolic visitor, Monsignor Maccari, could not have been more odious and inappropriate. Just think of the iron railing, which is still there today, around Padre Pio's confessional; for someone accustomed to those places, it seemed like nothing less than a prison. And then bishops and priests were prohibited from serving at Padre Pio's Mass; I believe never in the history of the Church has there existed such a prohibition.

Even worse: the Padre was required to celebrate the Mass in thirty minutes, forty at the most. This was really the height of ignorance and incomprehension as to what Padre Pio's Mass was, from the very first years, when celebrating in Pietrelcina took four hours.

And yet, in the midst of all this bedlam, although Padre Pio could hardly have been more embittered on the inside, he always sided firmly with the ecclesiastical authorities. To those who told him they had imprisoned and spied on him, he answered that he felt as free as could be; to those who complained that with these measures they had put him behind iron bars, he answered that everything had been done to protect him.

Woe to anyone who in his presence dared to advance a criticism against the ecclesiastical authorities and against the provisions of the visitor.

But I have to admit that there were two exceptions. The first was when he discovered the microphone; there he was taken by surprise and could not hold back his disappointment. The other exception concerned the duration of the Mass. He confided to his superior, almost weeping: "The Lord knows that I would like to do like everyone else, but I can't manage it. At certain moments, I am not capable of going on: I feel myself crumbling, and I have to stop. I will do all I can."

At this point, I prefer not to delve into the defamatory accusations made and the harsh measures taken against Padre Pio. I would have to talk about painful controversies that, at least in this brief profile, are better avoided.

Needless to say, the diehard followers of Padre Pio, disgusted in the highest degree, did not sit around twiddling their thumbs. Once again, they had recourse to the go-getter Emanuele Brunatto, who had never come across a door he couldn't open. But since all the appeals to the Church's upper echelons had been in vain, he turned again to the leading international organizations.

A "white paper" had already been prepared with a frightening amount of documentation, or, to be precise, with such documentation as to cause scandal. The paper was addressed to the governments of the U.N. member states; a conference had already been scheduled to present it, in the "Grand Salon" of the hotel Le Richemond in Geneva. But when everything was ready and it seemed there was no turning back, a terse order came from Padre Pio to call it all off. These were not the means he wanted.

This time, Brunatto obeyed. There is much about him that can be called into question, but in this case, his obedience was truly heroic. He knew he was embarrassing himself before the whole diplomatic and ecclesiastical world he had set in motion for that occasion, and he also had to use all of his skill to tear down the painstaking work of his hands. But he was able to make the will of

Padre Pio prevail: the will of a saint had to take precedence over human calculations.

Paul VI saw to undoing the actions of Monsignor Maccari and to guaranteeing Padre Pio's complete freedom. Already before him, John XXIII, who was full of affection for Padre Pio and had seen great harm in the measures taken for the purpose of clarifying the accusations, had said repeatedly during the last days of his life, "On Padre Pio they deceived me!"

12

THE FACE OF HIS ENEMIES

Padre Pio was loved dearly, but he knew very well that he had terrible enemies who hated him to death—not men, who may have been mistaken on account of bad information, prejudice, and incomprehension. The Padre never looked at any man as an enemy. The true enemies were the demons; enemies of the Padre and enemies of every one of us.

I believe Padre Pio's life brought to the forefront a reality in which many do not believe, because it acts under concealment. It is a terrible reality, which Saint Paul expresses as follows: "Put on the whole armor of God, that you may be able to stand against the wiles of the devil. For we are not contending against flesh and blood, but against the principalities, against the powers, against the world rulers of this present darkness, against the spiritual hosts of wickedness in the heavenly places" (Eph 6:11–12). Saint Paul's identification of the demons is very precise because he calls them by the names of the ranks to which they belong. I believe this, too, was one of the missions of Padre Pio: a clear struggle—that, for him, was even visible—against the true and hidden enemy, the dreadful enemy of all.

Many times, especially on television programs, I have been asked if I have ever seen the devil and how I would describe him. The devil, like all of the angelic world to which he belongs, is a pure spirit; not having a body, he is not visible or describable. If he wants to appear in a perceptible way, he has to use a contrived form, which he assumes on the basis of the effect he wants to provoke.

The same goes for the angels. When the archangel Raphael was given the task of accompanying Tobit's son, he took on the appearance of a young man dressed in traveler's garb; Saint Frances of Rome saw her guardian angel in the form of a radiant child, which is why she is depicted with a little boy beside her. Other angels have appeared in the image of a luminous being. This is always a matter of making their presence perceptible and not of the reality of their spiritual being.

The devil follows the same criterion. In order to make his presence perceptible, he employs an appearance that corresponds to the effect he wants to bring about: *fear, seduction, deception*. We have noted how Padre Pio, from his earliest childhood, enjoyed heavenly visions on such a regular basis that he thought everyone had them. But he also saw demons, almost always under appearances so horrifying that he was stricken with terror. And for the rest of his life, he continued to see the face of the cruel enemy under different appearances that always conveyed his evil character, although the perceptible form was not that of his true nature as a pure spirit.

Most of the time, the Padre saw the demons as horrible beings that tormented him, even striking him with noisy chains, leaving him bruised and bleeding. Other times, they presented themselves as horrid animals, loud and frightening. Padre Pio gave a very significant description of the demonic attacks to his spiritual director when he was at the friary in Venafro, where his superiors had sent him in 1911 so he could complete his studies and learn sacred eloquence [or preaching]. It was one of his many brief and distressing stays that ended with his return to his native air of Pietrelcina. It was in Venafro that Padre Pio's interior life was clearly manifested for the first time, in terms of both the demonic attacks and the ecstasies that often followed these, in which the Padre spoke freely with the Lord or with Our Lady, without noticing that another friar was there and could hear him.

The devil sometimes appeared in the form of an ugly black cat or some other repugnant animal; it was clear that his intention was to instill terror. Other times, he took the appearance of naked

young women who tried to provoke Padre Pio
with obscene dances, clearly tempting the young
priest to sin against chastity.

But the greatest dangers came when the devil
tried to trick Padre Pio by appearing in sacred forms
(the Lord, Our Lady, Saint Francis ...), or in the
forms of persons who had authority over him (the
superior of the friary, the provincial superior, his
spiritual director ...). In these last cases, Padre Pio
had learned a rule of discernment that he then suggested to some of his spiritual children. We find it
in the writings of Saint Teresa of Avila, although
Padre Pio may never had read the Carmelite saint.
How does one tell the difference?

When the Lord, Our Lady, or his guardian angel
truly appeared, the Padre had noted he would
immediately feel a sense of fear, of dread; but after
the apparition was over, he would feel a great peace.
When instead it was the evil one who was presenting himself under sacred appearances, the Padre
would feel an immediate joy and sense of attraction;
but afterward he would be left with a bitter impression, a great sense of sadness.

And in the souls who came to him, what did
Padre Pio see? Sometimes he clearly saw them as
the prey of Satan. In a few cases, Padre Pio shared
this with the person concerned, and only with that
person. I think normally he did not see the devil,
although he fought hard against him; he knew very

well that the main activity of the devil, to which we are all subject, is to tempt us to evil. Often during confessions, he would make gestures with his hand as if he were shooing something away. Perhaps he was praying to the Lord to set the penitent free from temptations or from wicked habits. Saint Alphonsus, who is a master on this subject, suggested that in certain cases, confessors should mentally perform a brief exorcism before proceeding with the confession.

I believe it can be stated with certainty that Padre Pio's biggest struggles with the devil took place in wrenching souls away from him, both in confession and when he was praying for all of his children.

As for his battle against the extraordinary activity of the devil, Padre Pio had special power and special discernment, as we see in so many saints, although he was not an exorcist and therefore never performed exorcisms. Many times, people thought to be possessed were brought to him, and the Padre responded differently, case by case.

I would say he had particular discernment in knowing whether a person was ready for liberation. One time, a priest came with two burly friends who were holding on to a young man who, at the moment of Communion [during Mass], would usually cry out and writhe to get away. When he saw Padre Pio, he began to tremble. The Padre looked right at him and said just one word: "Begone." In that very moment, the young man was set free.

But immediate liberations are rare. I remember one young woman who had to be accompanied at Communion time because she was greatly troubled by an evil spirit: she ground her teeth and rolled her head around and around. Padre Pio held the host and waited, saying nothing, until he was able to give her Communion.

Another time, Father Faustino Negrini accompanied a young woman, Agnese Salomoni, who was in the grip of a dreadful possession, "because she was the best girl in the parish" and a curse had been put on her. At the time, that priest, who was stationed at a parish in Torbole Casaglia (Brescia), did not know he was to end his long life as the diocesan exorcist. Padre Pio gave a simple blessing, which seemed to do nothing. It was the parish priest who saw the liberation through to the end, which took thirteen years of prayers! I believe Padre Pio had understood that it was not yet time to set her free.

Other times, the Padre gave advice to exorcists on cases entrusted to them. He did this with Father Cipriano from San Severo and with Father Candido from Rome; he encouraged and assisted his fellow friar Father Tarcisio of San Giovanni Rotondo, who wrote a booklet on this aspect of Padre Pio's life.

Padre Pio always obeyed the ecclesiastical authorities, even at the cost of heroic suffering, and he always respected and loved them. The constant struggle of his whole life was against the enemies of God and of souls, the demons.

If he saw them under many forms and was beaten by them, I think this was meant as a reminder of their presence to the unbelieving world of today. The external realities Padre Pio experienced and suffered are a pale reflection of the hidden realities, of the gravity of sin, against which all of us must fight.

13

YET HE CONTINUED
HIS MINISTRY

In spite of the firestorm of suspicions and provisions, in spite of the accusations and restrictions, even during the second decade of Padre Pio's passion, he did not ease up on his ministry, his dedication to souls. I can bear witness, and I believe many share the same observation, that those who were not on the inside, who came for brief visits, had no idea what was going on. His daily routine was as monotonous and taxing as ever. The multiple prohibitions did not make a dent in the numbers of the faithful who found in Padre Pio their confessor, father, educator, the one who knew how to make the crooked ways straight and put them back on the road to God. They did not notice the additional sufferings that kept piling up for him.

On this occasion as well, it was palpable to me how the good sense of the people is often able to attach more importance, following the teaching of the Gospel, to the good fruits it sees than to certain measures.

For my part, I kept going to San Giovanni and encouraging others to go. One day I was there with my older brother Leopoldo, a lawyer who was one of the pillars of the Catholic Jurists of Modena, and I shared my convictions. In the late afternoon, when the church was already closed, we were walking up and down the avenue in front of it when we happened upon our beloved Archbishop Cesarano of Manfredonia. After the usual greetings, he had a question for my brother: "As a lawyer, what do you think about all these people coming here?" His answer: "You priests, I don't understand you. The people don't pray, don't go to church, don't receive the sacraments. Here is someone who draws the crowds, gets them in church to pray and receive the sacraments. And yet this seems to make you angry. Instead of encouraging it, you do all you can to deter it. I don't understand you priests." We were not aware of the onslaught that this most worthy prelate, a staunch supporter of Padre Pio, was withstanding.

The extraordinary gifts of God, such as Marian apparitions or the presence of a man of God who accomplishes a world of good, should be received "with thanksgiving and consolation", as Vatican II affirms in regard to extraordinary charisms.[1] But

---

[1] Second Vatican Council, Dogmatic Constitution on the Church *Lumen gentium* (November 21, 1964), no. 12.

let's be frank: this is not what happens. Normally the ecclesiastical authorities, when confronted with such realities, react with an incredulity and a resistance that have nothing to do with prudence.

I could cite cases without end, but it should be enough to recall the senseless opposition of the cardinal of Lisbon to the Fatima apparitions, in 1917. It was only on his deathbed, two years later, that he expressed his remorse for having so violently opposed something without ever bothering to become informed about it. I have repeatedly had to respond in the newspapers, over the radio, and on television to persons who were going to pray in Bonate, Garabandal, Montichiari, or Medjugorje. My answer has always been the same: I do not know of any place in which it is forbidden to pray.

I have never understood the prohibitions against those who organized trips to see Padre Pio, where the people prayed, confessed, attended his long Masses, and received nothing but good. I remember the approach that Pius XII took. One morning, he noticed that the cardinal vicar was sad and asked him why. "I have an unpleasant duty to perform. I have to go to Tre Fontane and get rid of all the stuff that has the people thronging there." The pope: "What do the people do when they go there?" The cardinal: "They pray." The pope: "Well, let them pray!" This saved a place of prayer that remains popular to this day.

I also remember what one German priest told me. He had organized a bus trip for pilgrims to Montichiari (Brescia). His bishop sent him a note in which he prohibited this pilgrimage. The priest went to bishop and said, "Many of our priests organize summer bus trips to Italy for a vacation in the mountains or on the beaches; you give these your blessing and consider them an apostolate. I organize a bus trip to go pray, and you forbid me to do so?" The bishop thought for a bit and then decided: "Go ahead after all, and pray for me too."

I have never understood and never will understand the fight many ecclesiastical authorities, religious and diocesan, put up against those who went to San Giovanni Rotondo, as if it were a threat to the faith. This took attention away from fighting the real threats and only got in the way of the good.

To serve the Lord with gladness

The stormy times did not deprive Padre Pio of affectionate contact with his children or even of his good spirits, which were always on ready display during recreation time with the rest of the friars, who by this time included a few of his more eager spiritual sons. I do not hesitate to say Padre Pio loved much and was much beloved. He was fully aware of this and thanked the Lord for it.

One day when I was in San Giovanni, a very practical friend pointed out something I had not yet done. After confession, I asked Padre Pio, "Can I give you a kiss?" And he: "Nooo!" Before he could finish saying it, I had already planted a kiss on his right cheek and on his left. Once in my gumption, I ended up giving his beard a little tug. He laughed contentedly, even if he grumbled, "So now they want kisses too."

This brings us to the recreation times with Padre Pio, which he enlivened even during the toughest periods, his only concern being not to burden others with his crosses and to keep them cheerful during those moments of amusement. Padre Pio was a true artist in telling jokes and in consoling those who were going through a moment of sadness. I remember that one friar, who was more than happy to be in San Giovanni, was ordered under obedience to move to another friary. That afternoon, when he went to recreation, he was really down in the dumps.

Padre Pio, humorously imitating the voice and gestures of the provincial, started to lecture him: "Son, it is for your good that I ask you to detach yourself from this friary and to dedicate yourself to a new ministry." Everyone started laughing, and even that poor friar couldn't keep a straight face.

Some of Padre Pio's jokes had become famous. He was so good at telling them, accompanying them with the mimicry that is so typical of southern Italy, which makes even someone who has heard

them ten times laugh as if it were the first. Listen
to this one:

In a friary there was a simple brother who was
so good, but he had a huge fault: he drank, and
when he really got a skinful, he had no idea how
much foolishness he was spouting or how much
mayhem he was causing. The father guardian had
chewed him out many times in private and in
public, had made him kneel in the refectory and
in the middle of the choir, in front of everyone.
The brother promised, beat his breast, made big
resolutions, but then . . . One day he found himself
alone in front of the tavern. He looked this way
and that: nobody around at all. He went in, sat
down on a barrel, and was blissfully knocking back
a bottle of wine [here Padre Pio did his imitation of a drinker] when he felt two big paws come
down on his shoulders. The friar began to tremble
from head to toe. He could barely bring himself to
turn around, and when he did, he was horrified.
It was the devil! The poor guy started trembling
even more. He had just enough strength to say in
a croaking whisper, "What a relief! I was afraid it
was my father guardian!"

Telling all his jokes would take forever, and I'll
stop here to avoid repeating the experience I had
after talking about Padre Pio to a group of children. I
had certainly exaggerated, but the fact is that when
I asked one of them if he had understood who Padre

Pio was, the answer came back: "Yes. He was a friar who told jokes."

This is another, albeit secondary, aspect of Padre Pio's character that debunks the impression some have that he was a surly type, even if his concentration in prayer made him appear, in photos as well, serious to the point of severity. But that was a superficial impression.

A poor friar who prays

"A poor friar who prays": this definition he gave of himself has become famous, reflecting the deepest aspect of Padre Pio's life: his incessant prayer. Jesus admonishes us to pray always, without ever tiring (Lk 18:1), and Saint Paul echoes this, saying we should pray without interruption (1 Thess 5:17). In practice, following the teaching of saints and spiritual masters, we strive to make a prayer of all the day's activities, knowing this is possible only if some times are set aside exclusively for prayer.

For Padre Pio, this was not the case. In the first place, he slept very little and ate very little. But we have seen how, from the time he was a child, he had grown accustomed to an intensity of prayer that had become a constant need for him. The way he used time would be impossible for us: he confided more than once that he was able to do three things simultaneously. One of these three things was certainly constant prayer.

Those who lived alongside him remember him above all in an attitude of prayer: either in the choir area of the old church, or in the sacristy, or in the gallery of the new church, or in his cell, or sitting in the garden ...

He loved to repeat: "Books are for seeking God; prayer is for finding him." And yet even his prayer was a back-and-forth of contrasting sentiments; it was certainly not a form of rest. "I pray even though not a single ray of light may come from heaven"; very often there were moments of interior darkness, when praying seemed to be of no use. In exchange, there were other times when he set himself to pray and felt pervaded by such love for the Lord as to set him on fire. He was so habitually united with God that he often seemed distracted, staring off somewhere else even if he was talking with people.

Still, he was very attentive, but without letting this be seen; he would respond appropriately, but at times someone might be disappointed after getting the impression of going unrecognized among all the rest.

I remember one friend of mine who spent long periods of time in San Giovanni and then had to go abroad for several years. When he came back, he joined the others in approaching the Padre to kiss his hand or receive a blessing. It seemed that Padre Pio was not aware of his presence, so much so that he got a friend to ask the Padre, "Agostino is back. Are you glad?" And Padre Pio: "What am I, blind?

He's been here for three days now." It hadn't gotten past him.

In a similar case, one of his spiritual children who had not been to San Giovanni for many years got the impression the Padre had not recognized him and even asked him at the end of confession, "Padre, do you accept me as your spiritual child?" And Padre Pio: "Why? Up to now whose child have you been?" He had recognized him just fine. I think he preferred praying for his children to talking with them, if there was no need for this. And he admitted that he prayed quite a bit more for others than for himself.

It is also true that during his continual prayers, he received the gift of heavenly apparitions, especially after his daily battles with the devil. The most frequent apparitions were those of Jesus, of Mary Most Holy, and of his guardian angel.

His exquisitely tender prayers to Mary deserve a chapter of their own, like all of his Marian devotions. The rosary, which he loved to call his *weapon*, ran almost incessantly through his fingers. He wrote that he recited daily all fifteen decades of the Rosary at least five times, which means he spent five hours every day just on the Rosary. But his recitations went even beyond this, which is comprehensible only if one keeps in mind that, for Padre Pio, time was different than it is for us, because he slept very little but also because of his capacity to do several things simultaneously.

Padre Pio suffered the pains of Christ's Passion in his flesh and bore its marks on his body, but he also felt in his soul the sorrows of Mary, whom he rightly saw as the greatest martyr, the true queen of martyrs.

I believe I can say that Padre Pio, with a certain nostalgia for the seven years of nothing but prayer he spent in Pietrelcina, felt more and more as he grew older the need to pray in order to be able to carry out his "great mission". Already during this second decade of fire, the time he dedicated to confessions had been cut down quite a bit. Long gone was the era of hearing confessions for sixteen hours a day. I remember that one year in particular, I got the impression that Padre Pio wasn't holding up well in the confessional. I confided my concern to Father Michelangelo, who told me there was a different explanation. He himself had asked the Padre one day, "Padre Pio, couldn't you hear confessions for a bit longer? Here there are people who have come from a long way away, from abroad, and now they are forced to stay here for days in order to get to confession." Padre Pio answered him, "Dear Father Michelangelo, what do you think, that the people come here for Padre Pio? The people come to hear from the Lord. And if I do not pray, what do I have to give to the people?" It seems clear to me that as time went on, Padre Pio felt more and more the need to pray for those who were approaching him, or were about to do so.

"He is a man turned into prayer", someone who knew Padre Pio well said to me. Prayer was truly his breath, his sustenance, through which he lived in constant union with God, no matter what he was doing; in a union not only of grace but of true presence, of dialogue.

The need for prayer was also suggested to him by his constant sense of unworthiness; he felt he was a great sinner, in part because he had a clear understanding of his own frailty, which is common to all of us men in this life. On account of this, he always had the fear—I would say the nightmare—of falling into sin, of offending the Lord, of not being worthy of what he was doing (above all when he was preparing to celebrate Mass).

With these sentiments, he was always a great beggar for prayers; he urged everyone to pray for him. I had noticed that if I wanted to see him light up with joy, all I had to do was say, "Padre, I'm praying for you", and I did not forget to do this. He overflowed with gratitude, and it seemed as if he were saying, "Finally, someone who understands me!"

One of the reasons he felt such a strong urge to pray was that he had a clear preoccupation. It was his duty to become holy himself in order to help others become holy. And this was a preoccupation he tried to instill in others as well, above all in priests. I remember very well going to confession to him shortly after I had been ordained a priest. As soon as I confided to him that I was a new priest, he immediately said to me with effortless phrasing, as if he were repeating a little speech that he used on such occasions, "Remember that a priest must be an atoner. Woe to him if he needs atonement! Remember that well." Simple words that stated clearly what a priest's responsibility is and how he must watch over himself in order to be able to carry out his duty.

Our Lady of Fatima

It was a stupendous day when, on August 5, 1959, the statue of Our Lady of Fatima arrived by helicopter at the friary. Here I hope to be forgiven if I ramble on a bit, since I was there when it happened. I can tell the story on a human level, but the Padre was absolutely right when he said, "Our Lady came because she wanted to heal Padre Pio."

The fact that the Lord uses human means to accomplish his plans must lead us to attribute to God that which is the work of God, but it is legitimate for the human instrument to bear witness to what he experienced, even if he knows very well that this is a matter of things that are greater than he is. I do not know why the Lord has used me for certain works of great importance; the merit is not mine, but I recount the facts. If I had not gone with the necessary documents to ask Cardinal

Lercaro to become the sponsor, at the Italian Episcopal Conference, of the consecration of Italy to
the Immaculate Heart of Mary, this consecration
would not have taken place. I do not know why
the Lord used me to bring Our Lady of Fatima to
Padre Pio, just as I do not know why the Lord
is now using me to reestablish the exorcistate in
the Church, after it was practically abandoned for
three centuries.

The facts are these. I was a secretary of the committee for preparing the consecration of Italy to the
Immaculate Heart of Mary, scheduled for September
13, 1959, in Catania, where the National Eucharistic
Congress would be held. I found myself in a condition of great privilege. We had decided, in order to
prepare the Italian people for the event in the little
time available, to organize a great *Peregrinatio Mariae*.
The statue of the Virgin from Fatima was taken by
helicopter to all the provincial capitals. Monsignor
Strazzacappa, who, along with me, was a secretary
of the committee, had sketched out the itinerary in
one sitting (he had felt almost inspired). I can still
see that sheet, which was immediately sent to all the
bishops and accepted by all with gratitude and without objections. Time was of the essence, and every
day from the end of April to September had to be
used, without making distinctions between Sundays
and weekdays, and without taking summer vacation
into account.

A thought came to me: What if we made an exception and put a visit to Padre Pio on the itinerary? I looked at the calendar and noticed something unusual. Here are the first days of August as they were planned and then realized: the first, L'Aquila; the second, Chieti; the third, Pescara; the fourth, Campobasso; the fifth, Foggia; the sixth and seventh, Benevento; the eighth, Caserta; the ninth, Avellino ...

How in the world had Monsignor Strazzacappa (who loved to make fun of his own last name, "torn cape") assigned two days to Benevento? Didn't this make it possible to recover a day for Padre Pio, offered by none other than the province where he was born? So I wrote to the bishop of Benevento without specifying the reason, saying only that I wanted to treat everyone the same. The bishop replied immediately that he had no problem with giving up the extra day, which had puzzled him as well. So now there was a day for Padre Pio, from the evening of August 5, arriving from Foggia, to the evening of August 6, departing for Benevento.

I wrote to the Capuchins so that they could inform the archbishop of Manfredonia and let me know what they thought. Dear Father Mariano sent me an enthusiastic reply, on behalf of himself and the other friars. But there was one objection, and it came from the archbishop. In a letter dated April 15 (it was already 1959), he wrote to me that he did not think it was appropriate that on such a solemn itinerary, on which the only stops scheduled were the provincial capitals, an exception should be made for San Giovanni Rotondo; I would at least have to ask the Holy Office. At the time, I didn't know a thing about that decade of fire, in which Archbishop Cesarano felt caught up. I thought once again about resorting to the mediation of Cardinal Lercaro, and the Capuchins agreed with me. The archbishop of Manfredonia wrote to me again on May 4 to tell me that, after hearing from a prince of the Church, moreover one appointed by the episcopal conference as president of the organizing committee with full powers, he no longer had any difficulty and felt free from any responsibility.

This was how, on the afternoon of August 5, the helicopter with Our Lady of Fatima landed at Padre Pio's friary. It should be noted that on April 25, the very day the great Marian pilgrimage began in Naples, Padre Pio fell ill with effusive pleurisy, and by May 5 he was no longer able to celebrate Mass.

On the morning of August 6, with great effort, Padre Pio came out to honor the statue of Our Lady. There is a famous photograph that shows the Padre, assisted by another friar, placing a set of rosary beads on the hands of Our Lady. On the afternoon of the sixth, the Padre followed the departure of the helicopter from the window of the choir area.

He pleaded, "Our Lady, my Mama, you came to Italy, and I got sick; now you're going away and leaving me still sick?" At that moment, he felt a sort of shiver and said to the friars who were with him, "I'm healed." He felt healthy and strong as never before in his life.

14

A SLOW DECLINE

We can consider 1962 the end of the second decade of fire, even though it was not completely over until 1964. But it also began the Padre's definitive physical decline. If, during the first horrible decade, he had to undergo personal restrictions, such as the prohibition on saying Mass in public and hearing confessions, during the second decade he suffered under more subtle suspicions and monitoring, exemplified by the microphones and the prohibition on dealing with certain matters concerning his beloved Home for the Relief of Suffering.

The canonical visitation by Monsignor Maccari was very difficult, and in this regard, I am able to provide one detail I learned about from a reliable source: at the Vatican, they realized perfectly that the visitation had been botched and was a failure; the important thing now was to save face. How? To make the whole thing look like a job well done, they made Monsignor Maccari a bishop.

But we'd better get back to Padre Pio. In 1960, because of the continual weakening of his eyesight, he was allowed to substitute the recitation of the Rosary for the recitation of the Liturgy of the Hours. For him, elderly as he was and accustomed to celebrating with texts he already knew by heart, it was an enormous task to celebrate the Mass in Italian, having to learn everything all over again.

There are many highly authoritative Church figures who maintain that the stark rupture with the past was a mistake, even though they fully approve of the liturgical changes that were made. In any case, Padre Pio was allowed to celebrate in Latin, but often, from 1965 on, his health problems kept him from saying Mass at all.

From November 1966 on, the Padre had to celebrate sitting down. I remember well the pain it caused me to see him celebrate like this. His Mass, which, on account of his evident weariness, had become rather brief in terms of duration, no longer seemed the same as it had once been, now that he had to remain seated. And yet the suffering on his face, which became ever more recognizable as he lost the strength he needed to hide it, continued to embody the Passion in an evident way. Everyone was forced to acknowledge the reality: the physical decline was evident. It came as no surprise when someone found out what he had made a point of saying to one of his nieces: "In two years, I won't be here anymore, because I'll be dead."

What never ceased were his struggles with Satan, the "giant" he had seen in his childhood and against whom he always fought, and always won, even if he suffered the wounds of these battles. On July 6, 1964, a loud rumble was heard coming from his cell; the friars ran and found Padre Pio on the floor with an injury to his forehead, which had to be stitched up. The demon had banged his head against the floor, and a well-known photograph shows Padre Pio with his face swollen from this incident.

Even in the past, Padre Pio had never been afraid of death; on various occasions, he looked forward to it as a liberator. Finally there came a day that all of his spiritual children had been looking forward to: September 20, 1968, the fiftieth anniversary of his stigmatization. It was a Friday. He did not want any special commemoration, as had been requested of him. But his children had come from all over the world, and during those days, the church was always packed: an international convention of the 740 prayer groups was in progress. On September 21, the Padre was unable to celebrate.

The dawn of September 22 came. The church had been adorned with festive decorations for that Sunday. At his usual time, 5:00 A.M., Padre Pio came to celebrate his last Mass. It was clear he was exhausted, out of breath, about to die; but at his side the superior stubbornly insisted that the Mass be sung.

Padre Pio made it to the end the best he could. When he said, in tears, "The Mass is ended, go in peace", the crowd broke out into thunderous applause that seemed as if they would never end. He staggered and had to be lifted into his wheelchair.

After the prayer of thanksgiving, he asked to be taken to the confessional for the women. Did he want to die in the field in which he had labored? Then he wanted to say what he called "the last goodbye to my children", at 10:30, from the window of the choir area.

In the afternoon, to the happy surprise of all, he showed up again for prayer in his usual place, in the gallery of the big church. He was able to greet the crowd again from the window of cell number 1, the one in which visits from pilgrims are allowed. It was his last appearance.

He had said repeatedly, "When I appear before the Lord, I hope to be accompanied by two mamas: Mary Most Holy and my mama." Well then, looking at the picture of his mother in front of him, he said to the friar who was assisting him, "I see two mamas." And when the friar objected that he was looking at a photograph of his mother, he insisted: "I can see just fine. I see two mamas."

Right after midnight, when the eucharistic celebration for the new day could go ahead, he asked

Father Pellegrino to celebrate Mass. He confessed and renewed his religious profession. He passed away gently at 2:30 A.M. on Monday, September 23, 1968.

Then came the last offices of piety. His body was composed, and it was noticed that the stigmata had disappeared completely, without leaving any trace of a scar; this was considered important enough to be documented in writing and with photographs.

For science, it will always remain a mystery how these stigmata suddenly appeared, remained for fifty years, and just as mysteriously disappeared. The purpose for which the Lord had given them was finished.

The body was interred in the crypt, where it still lies, which had been blessed on the morning of the twenty-second without any sign that it would be used right away.

15

MORE ALIVE THAN EVER

When people started building the first guesthouses and hotels along the avenue that leads from the town to the friary, there was no lack of criticism from those who said, "What's the use? With Padre Pio dead, everything here is going to die." What happened was exactly the opposite: Padre Pio's death seemed to inaugurate a grandiose new development that no one could have predicted. Homes, guesthouses, and hotels kept springing up; many religious institutes wanted to build facilities there. Those who go to San Giovanni today can hardly find their way around on account of the huge complex of buildings that has risen up, in comparison with what was there before.

The Home for the Relief of Suffering has also never stopped expanding. It carries out a providential service and bears witness not only to Padre Pio's love for the sick but also to his intuition concerning the location. It seemed impossible to build on that rocky hillside and completely inappropriate to select such an isolated place, so troublesome to get to. Today the distance is no longer a problem, and the spot is just right.

But what is even more striking is the massive influx of pilgrims throughout the year. The numbers were never as big when Padre Pio was alive as they are now, after his death. What is it that draws them? No doubt about it: the presence of a saint, whose remains are honored but who is also appealed to with faith. To this day, people come to Padre Pio to pray, to go to confession, to attend Mass, to receive Communion, to adore Jesus in the tabernacle. Padre Pio's presence can be felt more than ever on account of the graces he continues to obtain even more than before, especially in the spiritual realm: people go to him for conversion, to change their lives, or to get a fresh boost for their spiritual journey.

But so many also obtain temporal graces: healings, solutions to problems that seemed insoluble, and material assistance, such as finding a job or a soulmate for starting a family together.

The presence of Padre Pio can sometimes even be felt in a perceptible way, by a variety of means. There are those who dream about him, and the words they hear in the dream come true. There are those who have an interior perception of him through which a doubt is clarified, a torment ceases.

But there is also something that was already there when he was alive and about which I have not yet spoken: his scent. I never wanted to see extraordinary things when I went to Padre Pio; it was enough for me to look at his life, at how he spent his days, to be certain he was a man of God. When they told me about the scent of Padre Pio, I believed them (there were many who talked to me about it, people who were completely reliable), but I never had the desire to smell it. And yet it happened to me one year that this scent washed over me repeatedly, strong, unmistakable: in church, on the street, in the house where I was staying. I couldn't help but believe the evidence.

Well then, still today there are many who smell this scent. It is a sign of his presence and protection. There are so many testimonies that it is unreasonable to doubt them.

I would be remiss not to mention a certain personal matter. Ever since I became an exorcist, I have always gone for help to Padre Pio, who spent his whole life fighting the devil and always won. And I have to say Padre Pio helps me, no mistake about it. For my part, I have not seen him again, not even in dreams; I have not smelled his scent; I have had no sensible sign of his presence. But many times the demon, through the possessed person, senses the presence of Padre Pio and cries out, "That friar, no! I don't want that friar! Send that friar away!"

I have already had quite a few cases of persons who had never thought about Padre Pio but resorted to my ministry as an exorcist; and then in a dream, or by smelling his scent, they realized Padre Pio was helping them on his own initiative, because they had never appealed to him.

I have gone back a number of times to San Giovanni Rotondo. The last time, I chose a day in December, thinking it would be the off-season and not too crowded with the faithful. Instead, there were many buses, many cars; there were really a lot of people. To give an idea, the midday Mass had to be celebrated in three places at once: in the old church, in the new church, and in the crypt, where the Padre's remains are kept. And still there were clusters of people outside the church, because there wasn't enough room inside. I understood the need to build a big new church, and I thought back on the criticisms of those who, when the church incorporating the old chapel was being built, kept saying it was going to be too big; something so large would not be needed. Today, evidently, the Capuchin superiors no longer prohibit their friars from going to San Giovanni Rotondo, and the bishops don't look askance anymore at priests who organize pilgrimages. There's plenty of anxiety over saints who are still alive, but after they are dead, the bishops don't bother anyone anymore, even though the reality is different: their lives are always an example to be followed and a severe admonition to those who do not observe the laws of the Lord.

I consider Padre Pio the greatest saint of the twentieth century. This I deduce in part from his worldwide influence, even though he exercised this from his little cubbyhole in the Gargano. I also deduce it from a fact that was very striking to me. The Lord has given me the grace, over my long life, to get to know many holy persons, some of whom have had beatification causes introduced. All of the persons with a reputation for holiness whom I have had the grace of getting close to, whether living or deceased, all of them have been in contact with Padre Pio: either by ordinary means, by going to San Giovanni Rotondo, or by extraordinary means, because the Padre went to them through bilocation or in another way.

Before laying down the last tile, canonization, allow me to leave a question mark over something for which I have never been able to find a satisfying answer, concerning the relationship between Padre Pio and John Paul II. The great admiration that this pontiff had for the stigmatized friar is well known. We know this from his visits to San Giovanni Rotondo, from the writings he left when he was a cardinal, and from the speech he gave in San Giovanni.

What we do not know is whether Padre Pio really prophesied to the newly ordained priest, "You will be pope; I see over you violence and blood." I have investigated this episode but have come up with nothing.

I believe only the one directly concerned could resolve the doubt.

It is, however, certain that Padre Pio prophesied the pontificate of Paul VI. While Monsignor Montini was substitute at the Secretariat of State, Padre Pio said to Angelo Battisti, "Tell him he should prepare to become pope." The errand was immediately carried out by that zealous spiritual son of Padre Pio, who worked at the Secretariat of State and was a close friend of the one concerned. As soon as it came true, Battisti hurried over to the new pontiff as he was coming out of the Sistine Chapel. They stood there looking at each other, not saying a word but understanding each other perfectly.

The canonization process

This time we are not talking about a disciplinary process: Padre Pio was given sentences but never a trial. Now we are talking about the process of canonization, slow and painstaking, as was foreseeable. I will preface this with an observation. The *vox populi* does not wait for official declarations but speaks out right away. On the contrary, in these cases the official declarations depend, in part, precisely on the *vox populi*, or the reputation of holiness; this is one of the requirements for the process to be opened and to proceed. The canonization process follows a procedural course bound up with many human factors, some of them contingent, of pure expediency. The *vox populi* instead expresses itself with complete spontaneity: the people began immediately to go on pilgrimage to Padre Pio's tomb to ask for his intercession; they set up 118 monuments depicting him; they named streets and squares after him. The *vox populi* is not concerned in the slightest over waiting for the ecclesiastical verdict, which serves only to allow public devotion. As for private devotion, I do not believe this could be increased, already being at the highest level.

A cause of canonization follows various procedural phases. The first step is the appointment of a *postulator*, who introduces the cause in the diocese in which the person lived. For a religious, it is always the religious family that attends to the proceedings. So it was that Father Bernardino of Siena became the postulator who sent the request to the archbishop of Manfredonia in 1969.

After the acceptance of the request came the examination of writings, interviews of witnesses, and the collection of all the material required. In 1980, after the diocese had done its part, the archbishop of Manfredonia sent all the documentation to the Congregation for the Causes of Saints.

After an initial analysis produced a positive result, the Holy Father signed a decree to begin the investigation of the life and virtues of the servant of God Padre Pio of Pietrelcina. This took place in 1982.

At this point, the postulator is to prepare a volume, called the *positio* (position or situation), to be submitted to the appropriate commission. It contains an account of the life of the servant of God, a demonstration that he exercised the Christian virtues in a heroic way, and responses to any elements that might lead to doubts or challenges. The *positio* for Padre Pio filled seven volumes.

His life also posed many difficulties for people in authority who were involved in its many happy and sad episodes, and the positions and behaviors of each had to be clarified, above all in terms of how the Padre had reacted in the various situations.

This was done, and the favorable judgment of the commission of cardinals was obtained in the summer of 1997.

Finally, the conclusions of the whole process could be submitted to the Holy Father, who, on December 18, 1997, promulgated the decree recognizing that Padre Pio had lived the Christian virtues in a heroic manner and proclaiming him "venerable". It also affirmed the supernatural nature of his stigmata.

There remain two final steps: after the recognition of a miracle, the pope proclaims the venerable person "blessed". After the recognition of a second miracle, he proclaims him "saint".

Padre Pio worked many miracles. But it should be kept in mind that, for the purposes of the cause, only miracles performed after death can be presented, and the presentation must be made only after the signing of the decree with which a servant of God is declared "venerable". I know well that, for Padre Pio, there is already documentation on various miracles worked through his intercession after his death. But only now, after the signing of the pontifical decree, can they be subjected to the strict examination of authenticity required in order for them to be declared miraculous occurrences attributable to the intercession of the stigmatized Padre.

This explains the patience and prudence that are employed in such procedures, which, let's remember, do not hinder in the least the popular private devotion that has spread throughout the world—a devotion that has now become public.

BY WAY OF AN APPENDIX

When I set out to write this brief biography of Blessed Padre Pio, and, in particular, when I was composing the remarks that conclude the last chapter, I could not imagine that just five years later I would have to add a little appendix.

It has happened, in fact, that the documentation of the miracles that took place after the signing of the decree that proclaimed the heroic nature of Padre Pio's virtues, by which he was recognized as "venerable", has allowed his beatification to move forward.

On May 2, 1999, in the course of a solemn celebration in St. Peter's Square, Pope John Paul II, in fact, enrolled the friar from Pietrelcina in the register of the Blessed.

Neither I nor the many devotees present in St. Peter's Square, as also in Pietrelcina and in San Giovanni Rotondo, could have imagined on that day that the Padre would be canonized on June 16, 2002. But evidently, as Sacred Scripture reminds us, the ways of the Lord are not our ways.

PRINCIPAL DATES IN THE
LIFE OF PADRE PIO

1887—*May 25*. Padre Pio is born in Pietrelcina (Benevento) to Grazio Forgione and Maria Giuseppa Di Nunzio. The following day, he is baptized in the little Church of Saint Anne and is given the name Francesco.

1899—*September 27*. Francesco receives Confirmation. He received First Communion that same year.

1903—This is a year of decisive importance. In a vision, Francesco learns that his whole life will be spent in the fight against Satan, but he will always win, thanks to special divine help. In another vision, his "great mission" is foretold.

January 6. He enters the novitiate, with the Capuchins of Morcone (Benevento).

January 22. He puts on the Capuchin habit and is given the name Fra Pio of Pietrelcina.

1910—*August 10*. Padre Pio is ordained a priest at the cathedral of Benevento. Toward the end of the month, he receives the invisible stigmata.

1915—*October 10*. He reveals that for years he has been suffering the crowning with thorns and the scourging.

1916—*February 17*. He goes to Foggia to attend a dying woman.

July 28. He goes for the first time to San Giovanni Rotondo, where he will stay for fifty-two years, until his death; he leaves only for military service.

1918—*August 5–7*. He receives the transverberation of the heart, which will continue to bleed for the rest of his life.

Friday, September 20. He receives the stigmata.

1923–1933—The first decade of fire.

1923—Rumors that the Padre will be transferred from San Giovanni Rotondo. Violent popular opposition. Prohibition, for a few days, against saying Mass in public.

1924—*July 24*. The Holy Office exhorts the faithful absolutely not to go see Padre Pio and not to write to him.

1931—*June 9*. Padre Pio is told he has been prohibited from celebrating Mass in public; he can celebrate privately, inside the friary. He is prohibited from hearing confessions.

1933—*July 16*. The Padre can again celebrate Mass in public.

1934—*March 25*. He can hear men's confessions again.

May 12. After a three-year ban, he can now hear women's confessions again.

1935—The twenty-fifth anniversary of Padre Pio's priesthood is celebrated without any solemnity. This had been prohibited.

1940—*January 9*. Padre Pio decides to build the Home for the Relief of Suffering.

1947—Work begins on the construction of the Home.

1950—The large numbers of pilgrims make it necessary to use a reservation system to regulate the turns for confession.

1952–1962—The second decade of fire.

1952—*March 11 and April 8*. The Holy Office reports on problems in San Giovanni Rotondo.

July 30. The Holy Office bans eight books about Padre Pio; friars are banned from distributing writings about Padre Pio and organizing pilgrimages.

1954—The Padre is banned from dealing with matters arising among the staff members of the Home for the Relief of Suffering.

1955–1958—The downfall of the banker Giuffrè, to whom the Capuchins had entrusted enormous sums of money, which went up in smoke.

1958—Padre Pio is placed under supervision and spied on, to the point where microphones are installed in the parlor.

1959—*July 1*. Inauguration of the new church.

August 5–6. Visit of the statue of Our Lady of Fatima.

1960—Padre Pio is banned from receiving women outside of the confessional, and there is a disastrous apostolic visit by Monsignor Maccari.

August 10. The Padre celebrates the fiftieth anniversary of his priesthood; thanks to massive attendance by his spiritual children and by authorities, the commemoration proves very solemn.

1968—*March 29*. Padre Pio is forced to use a wheelchair.

September 20. The fiftieth anniversary of his receiving the stigmata. His spiritual children come from all over the world to celebrate this occasion; international convention of the 740 prayer groups.

September 22, 5:00 A.M. The Padre celebrates his last Mass.

September 23, 2:30 A.M. The Padre passes away peacefully.

1969—The postulator of the Capuchins submits the request to open the process of canonization.

1980—*March 3*. The archbishop of Manfredonia sends the last documents for the opening of the cause of beatification.

1982—The Holy Father signs the decree to introduce the process, which officially opens in San Giovanni Rotondo on March 3, 1983.

1997—*December 18*. Pope John Paul II proclaims the decree recognizing the heroic nature of Padre Pio's virtues. From that moment on, he is "venerable".

1999—*May 2*. In St. Peter's Square, John Paul II beatifies Padre Pio.

2002—*June 16*. Pope John Paul II proclaims Padre Pio a saint.